30 DAYS
to COURAGE

by CAROLINA M. BILLINGS

with

DR. ELISA MAGILL, EAN PRICE MURPHY,
GINA DE LEON, JACKIE LAPIN, JENNIFER POLANSKY,
LAURIE SMITH, LEONA KRASNER, LIL BARCASKI,
MARIANNE BJELKE, MARLENNE DOSS,
MARSHA GLEIT, MELANIE HERSCHORN, MINDY GILLIS,
SALLIE WAGNER, SHIRA RAYMOND, SIMONE SLOAN,
SIOBHAN CUNNINGHAM, & STACEY HALL

Published by PWT Publishing
A division of Powerful Women Today
3 Centre St. #202, Markham, ON
L3P 3P9 Canada

Publisher: Carolina M. Billings' email: info@powerfulwomentoday.com

Limits of Liability and Disclaimer of Warranty

The author and publisher shall not be liable for the reader's misuse of this material. This book is for strictly informational and educational purposes.

Disclaimer

The views expressed are those of the author and do not reflect the official policy or position of the publisher or Powerful Women Today.

Copyright Use and Public Information

Unless otherwise noted, images have been used according to public information laws.

ISBN Paperback 978-1-7771146-8-8
30 Days to Courage by Powerful Women Today

ISBN EBook 978-1-7771146-7-1
30 Days to Courage by Powerful Women Today

CONTENTS

Publisher's Note

I am beyond thrilled to have the opportunity to expand the Mission and Vision of Powerful Women Today to Champion and Empower Women's Emotional and Financial Independence.

As you can see, 30 Days to Courage is a guide. What our Mentor Experts write about are the product of decades long continuous formal and self-directed learning, documenting, testing, failing, reflecting, and understanding. All this learning has been summarized into 19 inspirational and aspirational chapters.

To say that these 30-Day Challenges and the steps to achieve them will take 30 minutes, 30 weeks or 30 years is to begin to understand that life is organic and on-going. It may as well be 30 lifetimes.

The biggest takeaway from this book is the need to take AC-TION. It is knowing that there is only one person who has the ability to direct your life. That person is YOU.

GETTING READY TO GET READY

We begin by Getting Ready to Get Ready. We want to open your heart and mind. Acceptance is the greatest form of Self-Love. This is your moment. Powerful Women Today is a social impact global movement. The sisterhood is real for those willing to embrace it with an open heart. There are so many ways to join our movement and be part of the change that will take women to income parity, to emotional self-sustainability and self-reliance.

Yours and as many women in the world.

Big Love

Caroline

Photo Credit: Pheasant Lane Photography

How to make contact:
Publisher@PowerfulWomenToday.com

Getting Ready to Get Ready

15 STEPS TO AWAKEN YOUR EMOTIONAL AND FINANCIAL INDEPENDENCE

Whether you choose to work on one specific area of your life or many, know that each area of focus does not exist in a vacuum. One of the biggest reasons we think we self-sabotage, which is a very negative thought process, can simply be that we are trying to build one room in a house without considering how it fits within the whole design, both structurally and holistically.

> "
> *The biggest myth in life is that we have time in the future. The only time we have to be our best selves is now.*

It's important to reflect deeply on the next set of questions, independent of outside context:

1. Are you happy?

2. What are your goals?

3. How urgent are they?

The Three Cap Stones

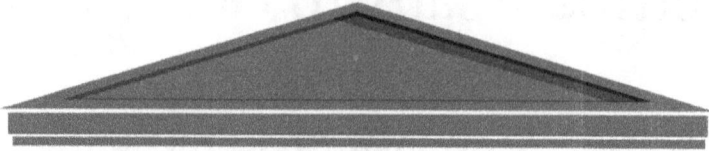

FULFILLMENT + TRANSCENDENCE + HAPPINESS

The Eight Pillars of Wellness & Success

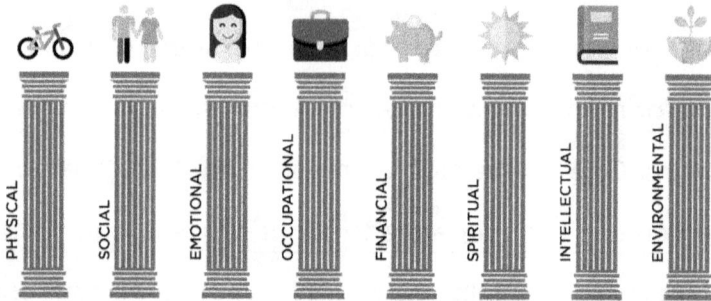

PHYSICAL | SOCIAL | EMOTIONAL | OCCUPATIONAL | FINANCIAL | SPIRITUAL | INTELLECTUAL | ENVIRONMENTAL

The Four Foundations

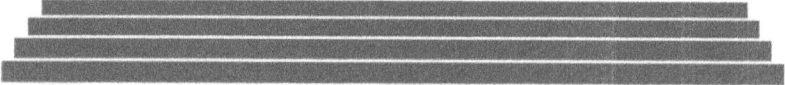

VISION + MISSION + PURPOSE + REWARD

4. What do you value? How do your goals align with what you value?

5. What does success look like? Do you know an example of someone who has achieved something similar to what you aspire to do?

6. What are your passions?

7. What is your life purpose?

8. What are you prepared to do to feel that you are the guiding force in your life?

9. What are you prepared to say no to?

10. What are you prepared to say yes to?

"

"Say yes and you'll figure it out afterwards."
—Tina Fey

WHY ARE WE DOING THIS ON PEN AND PAPER?

A written goal brings clarity and focus. It gives you direction. And by rewriting your goals you not only reaffirm what your goals are, you may also find new insights that bring more clarity and focus to your goal and life.

1. Writing things down helps you record everything that has your attention.

2. Writing things down helps clear your mind.

3. Writing things down helps clarify your goals, priorities, and intentions.

4. Writing things down helps keep you motivated.

5. Writing things down helps you recognize and process your emotions.

6. Writing things down encourages daily progress.

7. Writing things down enables a higher level of thinking, and therefore, more focused action.

8. Writing things down develops your sense of gratitude.

> **"**
>
> *"When you write down your ideas you automatically focus your full attention on them. Few if any of us can write one thought and think another at the same time. Thus, a pencil and paper make excellent concentration tools."*

One thing a lot of very successful self-improvement writers—Anthony Robbins, Brian Tracy, Zig Ziglar and so on—go on and on about is the importance of having written goals.

So, get comfortable, breathe deep and let's get started.

This is your *Before*. Do not read ahead.

Paint me a picture.

On a scale from 1 to 10 tell us (you and me) honestly how do you feel.

How do I feel when...	1	2	3	4	5	6	7	8	9	10
I feel happy when I wake up										

How do I feel when...	1	2	3	4	5	6	7	8	9	10
I look at myself in pictures										
I put my clothes on										
The phone rings										
I check my emails										
I check my social media										
I visit my family										
I get together with friends										
I tell people about my job/business										
I tell people about my dreams										
I check my bank account										
I open my bills										
I get into my car										
I think of God or Creator										
I pray/meditate/ dream										

How do I feel when...	1	2	3	4	5	6	7	8	9	10
I think of love for self										
I think of love for others										
I feel loved										
I think of all that I am now										
I think of all I can be										
I think of all I can achieve										
I think how others see me										
I think how I see myself										
I think how I see my partner										
I think he/she sees me										

30 Days to Courage

PART I

The Four Foundations

VISION + PURPOSE + PLAN + REWARDS

Without Them You Will Keep Doing the Same Thing Expecting A Different Result

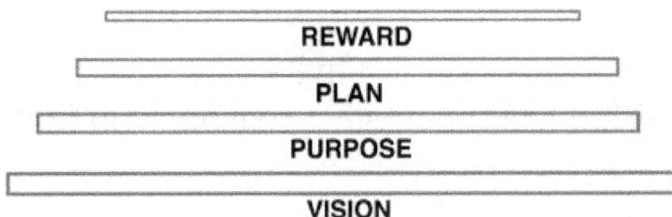

REWARD
PLAN
PURPOSE
VISION

There are many ways to set goals and plans for the future. Some are sound strategies like SMART. It guides you to make sure your goals are Specific, Measurable, Attainable, Relevant and Timely. These attributes for goal setting are valid. At least some of them. Absolutely, goals should be specific, but more often than not, time is not spent exploring and reflecting deep behind those goals. Knowing beyond what the final outcome you are wanting is as important as having the goal to begin with. I believe strategies like this keep you thinking small.

> "
>
> *"If you don't like something, change it. If you can't change it, change your attitude."*
>
> —Maya Angelou

So, I invite you to reflect on the two most important questions:

How ready am I to...	1	2	3	4	5	6	7	8	9	10
Change										
Do whatever it takes										

Why?
What are the biggest reasons you feel

#RadicalChange is needed for **#RadicalResults**?

Give me your top 5.

1 _____
2 _____
3 _____
4 _____
5 _____

Use the opposite page to write up the following Decision Grid:

What is the worst thing that would happen if I do what is right for me?	What is the best thing that could happen if I do what is right for me?
What is the worst thing that would happen if I don't do what is right for me?	What is the best thing that could happen if I don't do what is right for me?

What is the worst thing that would happen if I do what is right for me?

_____

_____

What is the best thing that could happen if I do what is right for me?

_____

_____

What is the worst thing that would happen if I don't do what is right for me?

_____

_____

What is the best thing that could happen if I don't do what is right for me?

_____

_____

Conventional wisdom tells you that to make sure your goals are clear and reachable. Each one should be:

* ❖ **S**pecific (simple, sensible, significant).
* ❖ **M**easurable (meaningful, motivating).
* ❖ **A**chievable (agreed, attainable).
* ❖ **R**elevant (reasonable, realistic and resourced, results-based).
* ❖ **T**ime bound (time-based, time limited, time/cost limited, timely, time-sensitive).

The problem with this is that it uses past knowledge which is limited knowledge.

Your goals and dreams should be so big that if they were to come true today you would poop your pants.

They should scare the living daylights out of you.

Why would someone want to live like that? Scared that if their dreams would come true, they would not know what to do. That, my Dear, is exactly the point.

I do agree your goals should be Measurable otherwise how would you know you have attained them. They should also be Meaningful and Motivating. Agreed.

Under Relevant it insists on using *think small* concepts. Reasonable and realistic are limited by what society may have taught you. What others have expected of you and what you may have allowed yourself to think. My wish is for you to THINK BIG. To want big things for yourself even if reality right now is telling you otherwise.

You need to be able to see beyond your current circumstances.

"

"Doubt is a killer. You just have to know who you are and what you stand for."

PART II

The Eight Pillars of Wellness and Success

EMOTIONAL + ENVIRONMENTAL + FINANCIAL + INTELLECTUAL + OCCUPATIONAL + PHYSICAL + SOCIAL + SPIRITUAL

YES, WE CAN HAVE IT ALL

We discussed the four foundations to awaken your emotional and financial independence. This is the groundwork and it's literally the foundation for creating your new reality.

When we think of success and goals, it isn't uncommon for us to compartmentalize. For example, our goal may be to lose weight or make more money.

However, even though it's easy to allocate a goal to a specific area of our lives (for example, in terms of money, we may think of career or business), the reality is that every single goal or pursuit affects every area of our lives.

The eight-dimension model was first identified in the 1960s as a theory illustrating the idea that all eight dimensions are interconnected.

This theory wasn't fully appreciated and embraced until the Wellness and Mental Health movements of the turn of the century, when mental health was recognized as a daily factor in

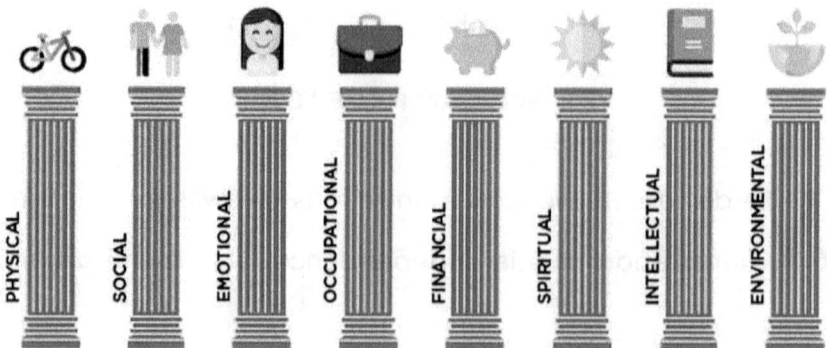

PHYSICAL SOCIAL EMOTIONAL OCCUPATIONAL FINANCIAL SPIRITUAL INTELLECTUAL ENVIRONMENTAL

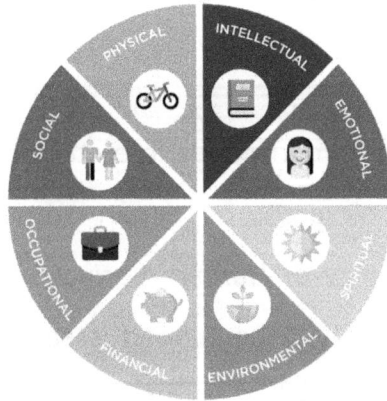

everyday life and not something reserved for clinical last-hope interventions.

In 1995, Dr. Margaret Swarbrick began to correlate and integrate all eight dimensions during mental health psychiatric rehabilitation research, later published in the Psychiatric Rehabilitation Journal in 2006.

In this research, Dr. Swarbrick explains that a holistic approach is needed to truly experience the lasting effects of trauma.

There is a significant paradigm in the field of public mental health practice that encompasses a wellness approach. Her research presented a holistic wellness approach by comparing it to the existing traditional medical model of isolating and treating symptoms without examining the root of the problem that may originate or cascade into different dimensions of one's personal life.

Instead of viewing human needs in a stacking scaffolding format like Maslow's hierarchy of human needs (proposed in his 1943 paper, *"A Theory of Human Motivation"* in *Psychological Review*), in which only once a need is satisfied can a person focus on the next immediate aspirational aspect of their lives each representing a smaller segment than the one below, a holistic approach understands that a need and its effects can occur and manifest themselves simultaneously across all aspects of your life—thus, the term "holistic." Dr. Swarbrick

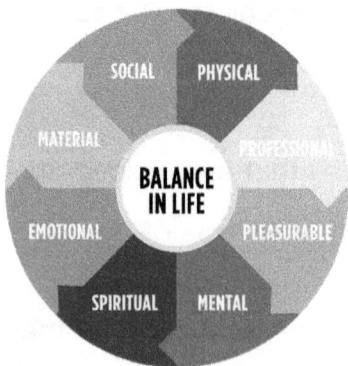

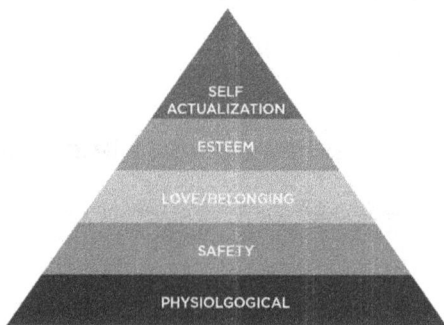

Consider this: When we feel financially stressed (e.g., increasing debt), we experience emotional stress (anxiety), sometimes leading to physical problems (illness), less effectiveness at work

(occupational), and perhaps even questioning our own meaning and purpose in life (spiritual).

When we aren't working (occupational), we lose some of our opportunities to interact with others (social), can't get the quality foods and medical care we need to stay well (physical), and may need to move to a place that feels less safe and secure (environmental).

I have had clients come to me because they were extremely dissatisfied with their jobs and wanted a mentorship to change careers.

In the process of doing a deep dive into the root causes, it would surface that it was the client's personal relationship and the frustration she was experiencing at home that was causing her to hyper-focus on her career—which she unconsciously felt was something she could control, unlike her relationship with her partner, which at the time she felt hopeless about.

Stress, addiction, trauma, disappointment, and loss can impact our mental health, our emotional wellness, and the balance in our lives.

> **"**
> *"You're going to be happy" said life,*
> *"but first I'll make you strong."*
> —Unknown

DOES HAVING IT ALL MEAN DOING IT ALL?

Success without fulfillment and happiness is the ultimate failure. Therefore, wellness and success are mutually inclusive aspects of awakening and experiencing your best self and creating your optimal life.

Wellness requires that we balance work with play and rest, that we balance time off for recuperation and recovery with living our lives fully and productively, and that we balance the desire for rapid change with the known effectiveness of slow changes to build good habits.[3]

The Eight Pillars for Wellness and Success are: (Notice how they are never listed in the same order, that is because they are circular, no beginning no ending)

❖ **EMOTIONAL**—Coping effectively with life and creating satisfying relationships.

- ❖ **ENVIRONMENTAL**—Maintaining good health by occupying pleasant, stimulating environments that support well-being.

- ❖ **FINANCIAL**—Being satisfied with current and future financial situations.

- ❖ **INTELLECTUAL**—Recognizing creative abilities and finding ways to expand knowledge and skills.

- ❖ **OCCUPATIONAL**—Finding personal satisfaction and enrichment in one's work.

- ❖ **PHYSICAL**—Recognizing the need for physical activity, healthy foods, and sleep.

- ❖ **SOCIAL**—Developing a sense of connection, a sense of belonging, and a well-developed support system.

- ❖ **SPIRITUAL**—Expanding a sense of purpose and meaning in life.

Awakening your emotional and financial independence is heavily reliant on identifying how your **Vision+Purpose+Plan+Rewards** fits into your future as well as being able to determine what your starting point is, and to integrate and execute the plan within the eight pillars of wellness and success.

Not only will doing this enable you to achieve a specific goal in one area of your life, but you'll be able to see how this one goal will fit into all areas of your life. A change in one will affect all, given that the composite of all is you—your life experience.

> **"**
> *Yes, you can have it all. That is, **your** all.*

REFLECTION: Visualization of yourself being happy is somewhat different than visualizations of more physical things (like your dream home, or money visualization, for example). It's used, of course, to manifest happiness in your life, but it's a fantastic exercise for learning how to attract that feeling even in stressful situations, when you're not feeling very satisfied with yourself or with your circumstances (you can read about how to "anchor" your feeling or state of mind in order to bring it back in whatever situation you need it).

Feeling happy will always help you in manifesting, because it's a positive emotion that adds to the strength of your thoughts, and helps relieve them of any negative connotation that may be hiding somewhere in your subconscious. That's why you can

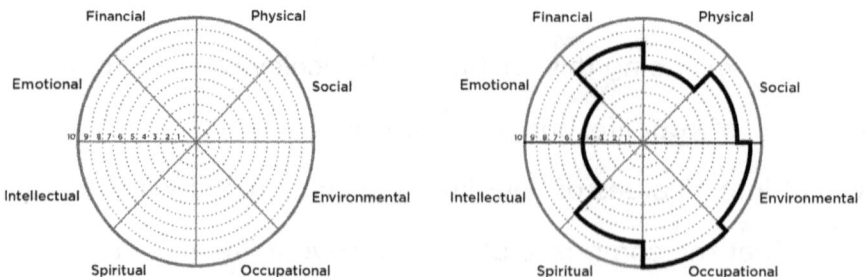

practice visualizing yourself being happy every time you're about to do some other visualization, as a preparation stage.

30 Days to Courage in Action

Self-awareness is the first step toward transformation. The Wheel of Life is a tool often used by mentors and coaches to be able to take a snapshot. A way for a client to check into their current state. It is quite simple, plot from 1 to 10, ten being the highest or best, as to where you are currently at. The image on the right is an example of one completed.

As simple it may appear, this is a great tool to examine what may be the roadblock. For example, someone that is feeling burned out may see their emotional wedge rated at a 5 of 10 such as in the example enclosed. If you notice, the occupational wedge is rated at a 10 of 10. This is most likely because you are spending all your energy on one wedge or area of your life, it is virtually impossible for it not to affect the others. What is amazing in this exercise is that the snapshot is so fluid you could do a check in in the morning and depending what transpired during the day your wheel may look completely different.

It is not unusual for a client I am consulting with 1:1 to come to me because they feel the need to change jobs and want a transition strategy.

When we begin plotting on the wheel it may become clear that other areas of her life are being affected. Perhaps the intellectual wedge doing a deep dive surfaces as the real point of pressure. It could be that it is not the job per se, meaning the company or the industry, or even the job itself. Perhaps it is not being challenged or feeling that you are not being given the opportunity to apply all your potential. So, instead of giving up on all the good will and seniority, we begin to put together a strategy to make a pitch for career advancement or an expansion of duties.

What becomes powerful is not so much the plotting. That is the first step. What really brings about goal achievement is the action forward. Taking charge of your destiny is one of the most amazing byproducts of empowerment.

HOW DOES THE WHEEL WORK?

It is recommended that you work with a coach or mentor at least for a few sessions to get started. I have created webinars to walk you through it if you wish to tackle it on your own. Let's say you plot spirituality at 3 of 10 and you have identified this is an area that you wish to develop. The question then becomes: What would make it a 4 out of 10. You then set up your goals for the week/month or set period.

The secret to success is that the answers come from you. It has not been prescribed or given to you with good intention by anyone else. In the example above, perhaps your answer will be to make a point to visit different places where spirituality is practiced so you find the one that resonates with you. You and your coach determine a reasonable time to check in again after you have taken action towards your goal. At the next check in, you rate it again and say now it has increased from a 4 out of 10. The question becomes what would make it a 5 out of 10.

Sometimes the wedge or area that gets identified as an area you are wanting to work on is a bit more complex or there is a

Example
TAKING A DEEP DIVE ON SPIRITUALITY

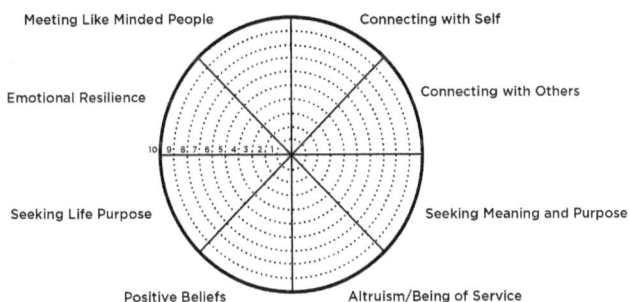

Meeting Like Minded People — Connecting with Self

Emotional Resilience — Connecting with Others

10 9 8 7 6 5 4 3 2 1

Seeking Life Purpose — Seeking Meaning and Purpose

Positive Beliefs — Altruism/Being of Service

need for a deeper dive. Each wedge becomes its own wheel. For example, with Spirituality working together you may identify which areas of Spirituality you are wanting to explore.

Remember it is extremely important that YOU help identify the categories for the wedges. We are trying to get to the bottom of your vision and purpose. There are no right or wrong answers. Visit our academy for more deep dive examples for each of the pillars.

TAKING-ACTION, is the most important step towards success. The simple truth is that dreams, visions and goals are achieved and accomplished only through action.

None of the theories and plans will work if you don't take any action.

> **"**
> *Dream it, think it, plan it, then do it.*

EXECUTION is the secret ingredient. Many people can have the same idea but what sets them apart is how they execute it.

Often times, someone is not sure about the best direction to take to implement their dreams, and therefore the temptation is to wait until the entire road map is available or the timing is perfect in order to begin.

So, it becomes a waiting game, waiting until all the pieces of the puzzle are available and make sense, waiting for the right conditions and circumstances, waiting and breeding procrastination upon procrastination—a procrastination infestation, over analyzing and saying that I will do it one day.

START at the level where you are, then grow and increase your skill level and output over time. Do something. Inaction is a killer of big dreams.

> **"**
> *The reality is that if you don't take-action to pursue your dreams nobody will do it for you.*

REFERENCES:

Graham, John "Life on the Edge"

Campbell, Joseph (1972) "Myths to live by" New York: Penguin Books.

https://www.divinecreativegroup.com/vision/

Fromm, Erich (1993) "The Art of Being" United Kingdom: CPI Group

Covey, Steven (2004) "7 Habits of Highly Effective People" New York: Free Press, 2004.

"

"I have learned over the years that when one's mind is made up, this diminishes fear; knowing what must be done does away with fear."

-Rosa Parks

"Here's to the crazy ones.

The misfits.

The rebels.

The troublemakers.

The round pegs in the square holes.

The ones who see things differently.

They're not fond of rules.

And they have no respect for the status quo.

You can quote them, disagree with them,

glorify or vilify them.

About the only thing you can't do is ignore them.

Because they change things.

They push the human race forward.

And while some may see them as the crazy ones,

we see genius.

Because the people who are crazy enough

to think they can change the world,

are the ones who do."

—Rob Siltanen

Introduction

COUR·AGE /'KERIJ/ NOUN

1. The ability to do something that frightens one.
"she called on all her courage to face the ordeal"
2. Strength in the face of pain or grief.

WOMEN AND COURAGE

There are two unquestionable universal truths:

"

"There is no wrath like a woman's scorn"

and

"

"There is no greater warrior than a woman
protecting her child"

I have seen both. I have lived both. I have been both. I have also seen, lived and been that same woman brought to tears and to her knees by what others thought of her. Paralyzed by fear to fail publicly, brought to tears by mean girls, gaslighted by a partner, betrayed by friendships and made to feel small by bosses, and even bullied by customers.

Women who give, who sacrifice for others, who do as they are told, are viewed as saints. Yet the woman who knows her value, sets her boundaries, and takes care of self-first is fair game. They, we, become a target for any entitled person to bring us down a peg, to put us in our place.

It is this societal rule that has created a mental jail for women. Why is it that being liked by others trumps liking yourself? Social Media and our celebrity culture with impossible standards -size 2 right after childbirth or re-entering the dating world only to find out men your age want to date someone who rock climbs Everest in 20 minutes, looks 20 years younger and is good with a hookup. Let alone entering into a relationship where two people take care of each other, you do you Darling. I am not saying this is representative of every circumstance, but it has become the norm.

In times of peril, do or die, women have the courage to be fierce, raw emotion takes over and a *Hulktress* emerges. Grasping every ounce of might within her. Yet every day, millions of us spend our lives conforming. Playing small, blending in, being liked. Not living up to our potential. Not living our best lives.

THOSE WHO SPEAK COURAGE.

There is a current trend within women speakers, thought leaders and influencers, to story—tell a tragic event in their lives to illustrate how they got here, to the stage of having the courage to share their story in service of others. Funny, you do not see a lot of men speakers doing the same. They may tell a great story to illustrate a point, but it somehow does not seem to have the vulnerability and raw emotion that women are prepared to bring to the ring. To genuinely leave everything on the mat.

Having the courage to share a part of you in service of others, that requires more than courage. Every time you retell a harrowing story your body, your cells, relive the trauma. Think, Prometheus was punished by Zeus because he stole fire to give back to mankind. He was chained to a rock in the Caucasus Mountains, and every day **an eagle** came and ate part of his liver. Each night, his liver would regrow, which meant he had to endure his punishment for eternity.

CLAIMING YOUR TRUTH IS THE GREATEST ACT OF SELF-LOVE

I used to look at survivors of great tragedies share their stories and say *"I am sharing so nobody has to go through this,"* and honestly, I empathized with their pain and their courage. But I must admit that once I witnessed first-hand the impact that sharing my journey, my pain, my obstacle has on others, I understood the sense of duty.

We are blessed to have among us no better guide than **Jennifer Polansky**, showing us with daily actions that *"The Courage to Love Yourself, Exactly as You Are A path to freedom, pleasure and intimate love. I think the most courageous thing you can do is look deep inside yourself, be with it fully, and love and accept exactly what you find. Rather than trying to change it or distract yourself, having complete trust that everything is working out for you, and to know that you both deserve and are worthy of that."*

Marianne Bjelke guides us through taking small steps to get ready to claim and own your truth in service of others. *"We all experience fear from time to time. There can be no courage without fear. If the thought of speaking publicly makes you nervous, you are halfway there! You can feel both nervous AND* *ready to speak publicly! When you finally step on stage, take a deep breath and get ready to captivate the audience with all the preparation you have done.*

Speaking is the best way to share your expertise, grow awareness about your brand, and gain new clients. And yet, speaking on stage, whether virtual or live, is something many people fear—especially if you have never done it before. Sometimes we feel more comfortable listening to others tell stories, and it can be hard to flip the switch and feel confident when other people get to listen to you."

TO ALL OF US IN FEAR, CONSIDER THIS.

We are guided by **Jackie Lapin** who invites us to *"Imagine yourself on stage in front of adoring prospective clients, all rapt, listening to your empowering words, and then eager to join your community?*

But there's a big gap from that image to where you are now? Maybe you're suffering from glossophobia (fear of speaking on stage)? Possibly you don't yet have a signature talk that you're confident about? Is it that you are reluctant to make an offer from stage because you fear rejection or believe that it will be too salezy? Perhaps you're just so wrapped up in your current business you don't have time to go find your stages?

These are all reasons that keep many women off the stages they deserve—and away from the audiences who need what they offer! Several of these reasons reflect a level of fear that holds women back!"

OBSTACLES DO NOT HAPPEN TO YOU. THEY HAPPEN FOR YOU.

Talk about courage. **Shira Raymond** teaches us there is no better time than now to reclaim your life no matter what age you feel ready to do so. *"Living in gratitude means truly being grateful for all the events in your life, and understanding that each moment has a purpose for your higher good. It also means that you need to stop blaming everyone or anything that might have 'harmed or hurt' you in the past. When we stop blaming others, we unclip our wings and can begin to soar."*

THOSE WHO ARE READY TO LIVE COURAGE.

Letting go of biases and things we think we know, **Gina De Leon** tells us how finding things out for ourselves first hand may be the key to unlocking potential we may not know we have.

"Over a decade ago, I embarked on an exploratory journey in Direct Sales to supplement my income. What I found was so much more!

I reframed my way of thinking and took myself from living as a single mom with financial scarcity to a place of comfort. Allowing me to travel, to provide for my son's private education, while enjoying a flexible business lifestyle! I'm so very grateful for this journey, and now for the circumstances that brought me to look beyond my then bleak, day to day, circumstances. I see myself in the mirror now and thank God that my life is unrecognizable from 10 years ago!"

HAVING THE COURAGE OF NOT BEING LIKED WHEN YOU STAND IN YOUR TRUTH.

"I am an acquired taste," is the reframing and transformation I experienced once I understood that my power lays in Emotional Independence.

"What good am I being liked by others if I do not like myself in the process or worse yet if I do not know or lose myself in the process. Being liked has made women compromise their values and compromise themselves for far too long. As women we should worry less about being liked. We should care more about

being effective, reaching and exceeding our potential. Most of all what we need to be concerned about is being respected. It is in bettering ourselves and bettering our performance that we begin to build the foundation for self-respect and achievements that lead to self-fulfillment....Our brains haven't caught up to the fact that we're not defending ourselves from wild animals any-more—so we continue to people please."

THOSE WHO DREAM OF COURAGE.

I am thrilled to learn from **Dr. Elisa Magill** that it is possible to awaken your courage. *"In today's society, we are taught from a very young age to stop listening to our inner voice, or as some would call it, our 'gut feeling.' Simply stated, we are taught to ignore our gut. To wait for... to follow others... to do as we're told, etc. As children, we listen more to our gut. We say our feelings out loud and without a filter, we are more transparent. That's why people love children and pets. They don't fake it and people can trust what they say more often than not."*

Owning your journey and having the courage to look back and reconcile can be as courageous as slaying dragons. **Mindy Gillis** is the epitome of grace and success. Championing and caring for those who care for others with the utmost grace and dignity. Yet her journey is on-going, recognizing courage under diverse circumstances is itself an act of courage.

"I used to be a very negative and angry person. My mother said that I was angry when I was born. Sometimes I wonder if I was a spoiled rotten princess in my past life and I was given a chance to redeem myself in this life. All I knew is that I didn't want to live in the same kind of circumstances that I grew up in. I vowed never to bring another person into this awful life. I have spent many years overcoming the barrage of negative thoughts that would flood my brain but would lead to anger instead of fear. I was angry for the life I was given. I was angry that life was so hard. I was angry with the family that I was born into. All of this anger came from my thoughts and perspective on life. Anger was my survival and coping mechanism."

READY FOR COURAGE.

Ean Price is teaching us that knowing your value meant having the courage to say no to clients who did not see your value. *"For me, that meant starting my own business so that I could determine my own income. I learned to ask for what I wanted and learned to say 'no' to clients who didn't agree with the value that I provided. That was the mindset work I had to do. But, when it came to keeping enough of the money I was earning* *to be able to pay myself, my expenses, and my taxes—that was where I needed a system."*

Why a coach and mentor will bring your best courageous-self forward.

COURAGE TAKES YOU PLACES YOU MIGHT NOT OTHERWISE GO.

Lil Barcaski frames it best:

"This year, I am committed to the concept of writing for the 'Greater Good.' This book is doing just that and I'm proud to be among this distinguished and caring group of professionals. The authors in this book are sharing their expertise, their techniques, their stories about courage.

We are all committed to giving you action items that you can implement week by week to raise your bar on courage, take your business to the next level, change your attitude toward positivity, gratitude, and prosperity. I promise you that if you write anything, a book, blogs, a chapter in an anthology, even social media posts, and you write from the perspective of how what you are sharing will help others, you will succeed. You will be thinking of the greater good, not just showing off or trying to make a sale or gain a new client."

EDUCATE, ILLUMINATE, AND ELEVATE

The courage to accept others as they are, not as how we wished they were. **Simone Sloan** brings thought leadership to the power of genuine and authentic inclusion of people different than us.

"Inclusion is striving to avoid treating others as part of a mysterious suspect, or as generic representatives of a larger group, rather than as individuals. Inclusion is making people feel they are respected and valued; that they belong.

Inclusion is a choice. It takes a lot of effort. It requires being intentional in our self-awareness and reflection; consistently re-evaluating our perspectives, experiences, and journeys. It also requires the courage to leave our comfort zone."

COURAGE TO RISE AFTER A FALL WITHOUT BITTERNESS OR RESENTMENT.

When you meet **Melanie Herschorn** you appreciate her sweetness and enthusiasm despite overcoming major setbacks: *"I hired a woman that I'd worked with in another capacity to help me. She claimed to be an internet marketing expert who could help me make my brand a household name. That was the beginning of the end of the company. She became verbally and* emotionally abusive toward me, constantly telling me that my ideas were boring and that there was no way I could ever do the marketing myself. But I felt stuck. She had me believing I needed her and I feared repercussions if I tried to sever our working relationship... After some introspection and talking with friends and my life coach at the time, I knew that I had to turn that awful experience into something positive. I found my voice and my mission again. When I looked back at my career up to that point, I saw that I'd truly developed a skillset to support women business owners with their marketing."

When all is said and done, the ability and desire to live our life to our fullest is the ultimate gift we can experience as humans. Women have far too long been held back first by the patriarchy, now unfortunately for many, by our own limiting beliefs.

It is time to change that after all

"
Fear is a reaction.
Courage is a choice.

Carolina M. Billings
Publisher, PWTPublishing
Founder, Powerful Women Today

"

"Courage is the ability to look at fear straight in the face and say: Not today."

—Dr. Carlos Munoz Barillas

Carolina M. Billings

Dedication

To my son Charlie my vision, mission, purpose and reward:

*the only **"like"** I strive for. And*

to my Father Dr. Carlos Munoz Barillas:

*The only **approval** I seek.*

30 Days to Having the Courage to be Disliked by Others but Loved by You

by Carolina M. Billings

> **"**
> *"Care about what other people think and you will always be their prisoner."*
> —Lao Tzu

THERE ARE NO "LIKES" IN LEADERSHIP.

Networking and referral expert Bob Burg is famous for his quote *"All things being equal, people do business with, and refer business to people they know, like and trust."* (from the excellent book "Endless Referrals"):

Being *liked* has far too often made women compromise their values and compromise themselves for far too long. As women, we should worry less about being liked. We ought to care more about being ourselves, being effective, and reaching and exceeding our potential. Most of all, what we need to be concerned about is being respected. It is in bettering ourselves and bettering our performance that we begin to build the foundation for self-respect and achievements that lead to self-fulfillment.

Our need for social acceptance grew out of our desire to physically survive—back in the day, we had to build shelter, find food, and defend ourselves every single day. It was all a lot easier to do in a group. To join a crew, you had to either have a skill that would benefit the group and/or be liked by people in the group.

Our brains haven't caught up to the fact that we're not defending ourselves from wild animals anymore—so as women, we continue to people please.

"

"In other words, we are hardwired to seek acceptance and avoid rejection,"

Let's be clear. There's nothing wrong with being liked. But the *desire* to be liked is what can get us into trouble. This desire to be liked, whether it's wrong or right, has a critical relationship to anxiety and to feelings of less than worthy by comparison.

The qualities we tend to like in women (modesty, humility) are not the qualities that get professional recognition, be it as an entrepreneur or in the corporate world. Qualities we tend to like in men (self-confidence, assertiveness, asking directly for what you want) are the same qualities we uphold in the business world. There is so much women can learn from men and vice versa.

Confidence, Assertiveness and Emotional Independence are the qualities that get us ahead in our careers. Leaders don't wait to be called on. They don't cower when someone disagrees with them. I would argue confidence is a skill, not a quality. It is more of a mindset and a way of life.

WHY SHOULD YOU CARE. WOMEN VS WOMEN

I have decided to graduate high-school. I am in my 50's about to complete my Ph.D. and somehow, I still find myself surrounded by high-school politics, mind games, and most of all toxic encounters... mainly with other women. This book has inspired me to take the courage to eliminate toxic people from my personal and business life once for all. There is just no return on investment.

I am the founder of Powerful Women Today. Its mission and vision are to Champion and Empower Women's Emotional and Financial Independence (Yes, I am a Treckie and don't care who knows it). From the time I was a little kid I was the odd duckling. I still am. Being a highly creative person I am in constant shift of interests, obsessions, and most of all research on a given topic. Empowerment of Women though is such a broad topic. You see, many women may find themselves empowered in one area of their lives, while feeling (or made to feel) inadequate in other areas by other people, by allowing and giving permission to be treated less than what we ought to accept.

> **"**
> *"In life you do not get what you deserve. In life you get what you accept."*

As women, we are taught from the time we are young to be pleasing, cheerful, and cute, to smile more, or that we should demonstrate boundless joy while doing almost everything we do in service of others. Women are even expected to be fun-loving while running for public office. When was the last time we heard a man's outfit being a topic of public discourse or how "tired" they look? Women who dare step into the public life as advocates or to speak truth are painted as difficult or nags or bitches; there's no lack of words used to mean "threatening woman." Men in charge are bosses, women are bossy. Men who are all-business are focused, women who are all-business are cold. Men are insightful, Women are depressing.

And, when the default expectation for women's personalities is sweetness and pep, it's easy to mistake seriousness and focus for nastiness. For women of color, almost any personality trait is labeled immediately as angry or emotional. Too many people don't seem to understand that women—who are human beings—contain a multitude of emotional ranges and are able to be serious yet fun, grumpy and loving within a short period of time (if not all at the same time), not because we are women but because we are human.

It's a mistake to confuse women's solemnity with anger; it's an even bigger one to disparage angry women. It not only teaches young girls that legitimate feelings are somehow "undesirable" —and that they should plaster a fake smile on anytime they're hurt or angry—but it also diminishes the importance of anger and taking serious things seriously.

"

To quote Tina Fey, "Bitches get shit done".

You might, in fact, catch more flies with honey, but what if you're more interested in raising your kids and keeping the roof over your head and food on the table? Focused and no-nonsense women are strong and capable and smart and aren't keen to be walked all over or care about being talked all over. Afterall, I am interested in the success of my business and career, not on flies.

> "
>
> *"What you think of me is none-of-my-business."*

Women have plenty to be angry about, in fact I am shocked that not more of us are saying: enough! It's not as if the world is a joy-filled wondrous place for us—we still have to deal with discrimination and violence at epidemic levels.

So instead of worrying too much about how I come across to other people, I try to channel my father and embrace my most caustic-self instead. I come from a long line of successful awful bed-side manner men who are admired for their focus and success, and a long line of messaging *"your value is only as pretty as you are, as thin as you are, as gracious and accommodating as you are"* from women and for women. Culture and upbringing for some of us is also a barrier to success that we must break.

The thing is, it is not only men looking to put "threatening women down." As a matter of fact, most modern men appreciate and respect a strong woman, especially in business. You will be surprised how many men wish their personal partners were also more astute and strategic. I have encountered this personally, many men when they see our company name Powerful Women Today and find out what we are about often say *"I need my daughters to hear this,"* or *"Can I send my wife to you?"* and other statements of support. Mainly because our movement champions and empowers women to take responsibility with actions, not condemnation or victimhood.

WHAT IS THE SECONDARY GAIN FOR WOMEN TO PLAY SMALL?

People-pleasing, approval-seeking, need-to-be-liked syndrome—call it what you will, but seeking self-worth through the approval of others is a fruitless endeavor and an exhausting way to go through life.

So why do we do it? Why do we allow what others think of us to have so much power over how we feel about ourselves? If it's true that you can't please all people all of the time, wouldn't it make sense to stop trying?

Unfortunately, sense often isn't driving our behavior. For social beings who crave love and belonging, wanting to be liked and caring about the effect we have on others is healthy and allows us to make connections. However, where we get into trouble is when our self-worth is contingent upon whether we win some-one's approval or not.

"The need to feel 'okay,' liked, or approved-of is rooted in the messages a person received about their inherent worthiness and belonging while growing up," says clinical psychologist Erika Martinez. *"Somewhere along the way, people with con-tingent self-worth learned that their worth came from others' approval, not from within themselves."*

> **"**
> *It is ok to be disliked by others. The only person whom you should seek approval is yourself.*

CREATING A LIFE WORTH LIVING & LIVING YOUR BEST LIFE

Imagine how much time we lose each moment we squash our authentic selves in an effort to be liked. If we base our inherent worth on the fleeting opinions of others, we cheat ourselves of the power with which we were born—the power to shape our experiences and embrace life in our brief time here with compassion—not only for others but also for ourselves. Be-cause ultimately, there is no difference. Embrace the cliché and love yourself. It's highly doubtful that you will regret it. Here are three tips to get started:

1. Cultivate awareness. Cultivate Yourself.

"In order to change unhealthy approval-seeking behaviors, we have to become aware of them," says psychotherapist Santiago Delboy. *"Sometimes they can be apparent, such as when we actively seek validation or avoid confrontation. Sometimes they can be subtler, for instance [when we] are very compliant, agreeable, or do not want to 'rock the boat.'"*

So, how do we recognize when we are engaging in these less apparent types of people-pleasing behaviors? Jenn Kennedy, LMFT, suggests asking yourself the following questions: *"Did you say yes when you really wanted to say no? Did you quiet your voice because it didn't please or echo someone else who you deem important? Does it seem like you are overextending?"* *"If so,"* she says, *"try pushing back on these habits and see what comes of it."*

2. Practice ~~self-compassion~~, make that Self-Acceptance

As an empowered woman within Powerful Women Today, one of the first principles we learn is to meet our clients where they are. This same principle should be applied to ourselves. The word self-compassion is often used to mean self-love. When

www.powerfulwomentoday.com

in fact it is not compassion but acceptance that empowers us. Empowerment involves accepting where you are in your life and who you are—flaws and all. *"Instead of being harsh with ourselves, it is very important to give ourselves the love, constancy, and security that we didn't receive growing up."*

An inextricable part of developing self-acceptance is caring for one's self. Self-care as the antidote to an excessive need for approval: *"It is speaking up when wronged, acknowledging accomplishments to self, as well as tolerating the discomfort of being dismissed or criticized. It's accepting that you aren't for everyone, and that is okay."*

"

In fact, self-care is the greatest form of self-love.

Part of self-care is putting ourselves before another—not in a selfish way, but in the way a mother must put the oxygen mask on herself first to be able to help her child. Without our own oxygen, we are no good to anyone else.

3. Build a positive support network.

A place not to be liked but to grow together. Who we choose to surround ourselves with can greatly impact our well-being and influence our sense of selves. This is especially true for those who struggle with where to begin. *"Since the need to be liked often stems from failures in our early relationships, it is important to develop healthy and reparative relationships."*

"These take time and require us to take the risk of opening up and being vulnerable. We might be afraid that by opening up we might be giving people more reasons not to like us." Even if that risk is fair, the reward is a nurturing relationship that can change us from within.

Being with people who are supportive of us for *who* we are, not what we can do, have done, or who we know. This helps us start detangling our self-worth from external outcomes, such as winning the approval of others. The sisterhood is real and empowerment circles are psychological safe places to make dreams come true.

> **"**
> *Remember that most of the time it's more about them than it is about you.*

Barring some egregious behavior on our part, a great majority of the time, another's dislike of us is more of a reflection on *them*. If we see something in another person that we don't like about ourselves, we often project. Projection is a defense that we all use to avoid facing the not-so-pretty parts of ourselves.

It often explains what happens when someone meets us for the first time and immediately takes a dislike to us or makes a snap judgment without getting to know us. Those who have higher self-esteem and feel more secure with themselves tend to do this less.

LIVE YOUR BEST LIFE

Join our Powerful Women Today Boutique Accelerator: *"Empowerment as a lifestyle,"* all about learning to put yourself first, to honor your values, goals and ambitions. Living your best life, right here right now. A life of Emotional and Financial Independence is not only possible, it is waiting for you.

REFERENCES:

Holiday, Ryan (2014). "The Obstacle is the Way" Penguin Publishing

Kishimi I & Koga F. (2013) "The Courage to be Disliked" Simon & Schuster

Campbell Joseph (2004) "Pathways to Bliss" New World Library

ABOUT THE AUTHOR

CAROLINA BILLINGS, PhD (C), MA-IS, CHRL, SHRP-SCP, CPCC is a social impact entrepreneur with 15+ year's leadership experience in the fields of Business Development, Leadership, Branding, Human Resources and Finance.

Carolina is the founder of Powerful Women Today, a boutique accelerator for success. A forum for the empowerment and optimization of women's status and lives.

Her sold-out conferences, publications, social impact, and Diversity, Inclusion & Equity initiatives have received the continued support and accolades of key champions of women in business. Carolina is proud to call herself an advocate working wholeheartedly for the emotional and financial independence and prosperity of women and their dependents.

Her Boutique Management Consulting Firm is comprised of elite experts championing women's growth. Her **#1MillionWomenChallenge** aims at positively impacting 1 Million Women every year to bring awareness to end violence against women and strengthen mental health and end financial dependency.

She is a leader with global impact who Champions and Empowers Women's Emotional and Financial Independence. She is proud of her adoptive home in Canada and is proud of her Hispanic heritage. She is a highly active advocate and champion of Social Justice, Diversity, Inclusion and Equity.

Carolina's dream is for every woman and little girl to realize that their uniqueness is their beauty and their talents their magic to love, touch lives, inspire others and shine brightest always.

CONTACT INFORMATION

Carolina Billings
Powerful Women Today ™
Founder and CEO
carolina@powerfulwomentoday.com
https://www.linkedin.com/in/carolinabillings
www.powerfulwomentoday.com

"

"She was powerful not because she wasn't scared but because she went on so strongly, despite the fear."

-Atticus

Dr. Elisa Magill

Dedication

This chapter is dedicated to my husband, James Magill, for both listening to and understanding my "idea rambling," and continually encouraging me to follow my dreams!

The Empowered You!

OUR CONNECTION BETWEEN THOSE 'GUT FEELINGS' AND PERSONAL STRENGTH

by Dr. Elisa Magill

Mary was super excited and full of hope, she was just promoted at her company and was starting her first day as the new Executive Director of Marketing. She was even grateful for the new home that her company paid for as she had to move out of state to start this new position. Everything was set up and ready to go,it was perfect. She was ready! Having been at her company for the past ten years, Mary felt she had a really good grip on what was needed and the direction she wanted to go.

With renewed vigor, on day one of her new position, she confidently walked into the conference room to greet her new team. She whole-heartedly shared her strategic marketing plan, expecting to elicit more excitement from the team. However, instead of feeling their excitement and commitment to the plan, Mary detected that something was wrong, there seemed to be a disconnect between what they were saying and the "vibe" she was picking up on. They were all smiles, saying they were on board and felt good about her direction, but she thought she detected a bit of discontent, and even a bit of resentment from some of them. When she asked her boss, who was there to introduce her on her first day, he said that she was doing great and that they were all on board. Mary took that as confirmation that all was well and dismissed the team to begin on the new project. Eventually, the project tanked and the complaints started to roll in. As the disconnect started to surface, Mary sat back, reflecting on the past several months. She then connected the dots and thought, *"I knew it! I thought something was wrong. Why did I ignore it back then? I should have dug deeper."*

What Mary experienced above is not unusual. In fact, most of you reading this book (including myself) have felt this way at one time or another. It goes back to the popular saying that "Hindsight is 20/20." Meaning that things become crystal clear after the plan has been rolled out, since all areas of concern are now obvious. But, is it possible to adjust and correct things before they fall apart as they did in Mary's example above? Yes, it is possible! Which begs the question...how and why?

To answer that question, let's reflect on what happened at the start of Mary's story. In the beginning, she was excited. She felt she had a good grip on things and great ideas. Her perception of her new team was that they would be on board, and if they were not, they would be open with her like her previous team was. She trusted her new boss, as they already had a working professional relationship with each other, and she trusted the process. What she realized in hindsight, was that she failed to trust herself... or her inner voice. Something was tugging at her, alerting her to the fact that the energy felt did not match what was being said. In other words, the nonverbal communication did not match the verbal communication. Since it is believed that 93% of communication is nonverbal (Weiss, 2016), it is vital to truly understand what is being said, or to even decipher an underlying issue that no one has identified or is aware of yet.

Even though the "how" is explained above, you may be asking "why" is this still a problem? In today's society, we are taught from a very young age to stop listening to our inner voice, or as some would call it, our "gut feeling." Simply stated, we are taught to ignore our gut. To wait for... to follow others... to do as we're told, etc. As children, we listen more to our gut. We say our feelings out loud and without a filter, we are more transparent. That's why people love children and pets. They don't fake it and people can trust what they say more often than not.

Currently, adults are being told the same thing. *"Do it like this because it works,"* but does a "one size fits all" mentality work? Or does it depend on the person or the situation? In most situations, it depends. At other times, people end up jumping on the bandwagon, so to speak. They do it, as it is the popular thing to do, but sometimes it doesn't feel right and they are not sure why (Areni, Ferrell, & Wilcox, 2000). Learning to listen to and decipher our gut will help us to become free of the *"I'm not sure why I feel this way"* syndrome and will help us to not ignore important "data" that our senses picked up on, which will help us to make more informed decisions.

However, some may wonder, *"Well, if the person telling me what to do is successful and knowledgeable, shouldn't I just do as I am told?"* Although this may work well in some situations, it may not always be the best solution. This is especially true if the individual/s who are involved are ignoring their gut instincts. This is not to say listening to an expert is wrong. Instead, it is failing to also listen to our inner voice that is wrong. Most of the time, that inner voice (or our gut feeling) is what helps us pick up on those nonverbal cues, that additional "data" that would be otherwise missed. To only listen to what is written or known and ignore the rest is like asking a computer to tell you how it feels. It is logic without emotion. It is regurgitation of what is known or processed, minus the human factor. If we are going to work with humans in any way, shape, or form, we need to understand emotions. This is because we are social beings with emotions at the core of all our decisions. This does not mean we are "emotional" as some understand this word (i.e. out of control), but we are emotional beings in that we feel, care, are compassionate, and have a feeling attached to the decisions we make (Goleman, 1998).

In summary, we need to pay attention to this energy zapping gap between what we're doing now and what we should be doing. The solution presented to us currently in today's society (just do it like this) is not always a right fit for what we feel and for what we are going through based on our personal values, beliefs, and desires/needs. By not listening to our gut, we are missing important data that can give us a clear picture of what we are facing. To get all the data, and make a well-informed decision, we need to listen to our gut. Only then can we truly feel empowered!

As shared above, the solution to this problem of incongruence lies in connecting with and listening to our gut...the data we need to make more informed decisions. If we do this, we can minimize feelings of disconnect with what we feel is right and what we are doing. Festinger coined this Cognitive Dissonance, where we cannot hold two incompatible beliefs together in our minds at the same time. We will end up pushing one down in importance so that we can entertain the other (Manis, 1978).

If both thoughts/ideas are equally important to us, this can be hard to do. If one thought/idea is incongruent with a personal belief/value that we have, this will be hard to do. It will not sit well in our hearts and minds and can lead us to be disengaged and discouraged in what it is we are setting out to do. This will also end up draining our energy. It can even demotivate us to the point where we may sabotage our own success since, inwardly, we are not excited or fully united with what we have planned. If we address this early on, we will become more congruent with what we're doing in life and business and will experience less resistance, less frustration, and improved business results/efficiencies. What happens then? We strengthen our core from the inside out. We become more resilient, more excited, and more motivated. We become ready for action and can then endure whatever comes our way. This is the recipe for true personal power that will help us achieve lasting results that lead to a successful return on investment. One that leaves a legacy we can be proud of!

Okay... I'm ready to listen to my gut!

If you get what is explained above, then you may be ready to practice listening to your inner voice more often. Here is a simple plan that can get you moving forward in just 30 days or less. I'd suggest journaling what you discover each day. Then, focus on making positive changes, one tiny step at a time.

STEP ONE: REFLECTION

Reflect on 3 major decisions you made in your life. Analyze the past... have you felt that way before? Were you right? What is your "Hindsight is 20/20" story?

Answer the following questions:

1. What elements did you consider when you made your decision?

2. How long did you give yourself to make the final decision after gathering your facts and/or thinking it over?

3. Did you ask others their opinion?

4. Was there a moment when someone suggested you do things one way, but something was telling you not to do it that way? Did you listen to them? Or adjust things based on your personal feelings/thoughts or insights on the matter?

5. What would you have done differently and why?

6. What are you happy you did and why?

In answering these questions, start to look for patterns. Pay attention from this point on to how you make decisions, or how you engage in your everyday work plans. What moods do various activities give you? Do you avoid these activities? Run toward them? What puts you into the "spin cycle," where you feel overwhelmed, burned out, and disengaged? What do you think you could do differently? In other words, what energizes you (empowers you)? What discourages or drains you? Once you identify these, you can start to adjust your behavior to achieve more satisfying and empowering results.

STEP TWO: AWARENESS

On top of reflecting on past behaviors, pay attention to how you feel in the present moment. Is there a shift in your energy or level of excitement? If so, is there a connection between events or a trigger that gets you feeling this way?

How does staying aware empower you? If you can identify what pulls you down and what picks you up, you can plan to work around the downward spiral and work on staying on track more often than not. When we do this, we are strengthening ourselves and increasing our personal power and endurance in life and business. This will also help you to think of possible solutions ahead of time, helping you to manage your emotions or know when to draw the line in life and business.

STEP THREE: PAYING ATTENTION TO YOUR GUT!

In a nutshell, this means LISTEN TO ALL OF THE CUES! Instead of looking back and saying, *"I knew it!"* Look back and say, *"Thank God I listened to my gut!"* Interestingly, emotional intelligence research shows that our organs act as data collectors. They pick up on external energy and transfer that data to the logical centers of our brain (where we make decisions). In summary, our brain and body are connected and to get the full picture of what is happening, we need to listen to both (Goleman, 1998). This means that our whole body works together as an efficient communication system. If we block out listening to one part, we are working with faulty equipment. Therefore, stop, take a breath, and think about how you feel when presented with an issue. Listen inwardly. If you feel a hesitation, dig deeper, try to identify why you feel that way. If you feel excited, what is it about that situation that is boosting your energy?

How would it feel to begin or continue on a path that just felt right? One you were excited to embark on? One where you weren't hesitant because something felt "off?" By engaging in personal reflection, awareness, and listening to those gut feelings, we can choose to live with courage, conviction, and energy... to live the OPTIMAL YOU!

REFERENCES

Areni, C. S., Ferrell, M. E., & Wilcox, J. B. (2000). The persuasive impact of reported group opinions on individuals low vs. high in need for cognition: Rationalization vs. biased elaboration? *Psychology & Marketing*, 17(10), 855-875. https://2q21c-jvnp-mp01-y-https-www-proquest-com.proxy.lirn.net/scholarly-journals/persuasive-impact-reported-group-opinions-on/docview/227688273/se-2?accountid=150887

Goleman, D. (1998). *Working with emotional intelligence*. New York, NY: Bantam Books

MANIS, M. (1978). Cognitive social psychology and attitude change: COGNITIVE SOCIAL PSYCHOLOGY BALANCE THEORY COGNITIVE DISSONANCE LOGIC AND SOCIAL COGNITION ATTRIBUTION THEORY COGNITION AND ATTITUDE CHANGE SOURCE-AND AUDIENCE-EFFECTS INVOLVEMENT ATTITUDES AND BEHAVIOR REFERENCES. *The American Behavioral Scientist* (Pre-1986), 21(5), 675. Retrieved from https://2q21cjvqr-mp01-y-https-www-proquest-com.proxy.lirn.net/scholarly-journals/cognitive-social-psychology-atti-tude-change/docview/194630524/se-2?accountid=150887

Weiss, W. (2016). What are you really communicating? *Life-HealthPro,* https://2q21cjvnp-mp01-y-https-www-proquest-com.proxy.lirn.net/trade-journals/what-are-you-really-commu-nicating/docview/1789093065/se-2?accountid=150887

ABOUT THE AUTHOR

DR. ELISA MAGILL is the CEO of Endurance Business Builders and the Academy for Transformational Success, specializing in harnessing ones' personal energy, performance improvement, distraction management, and creating a business that endures the test of time while avoiding burnout. Elisa combines her Ph.D. in Industrial/Organizational Psychology, and MBA in Executive Management and Entrepreneurship with her decades of applied experience centered around emotional intelligence and resiliency research to support and empower her clients to ignite their dreams and *"Make it Happen Now!"* Elisa is the Amazon best-selling author of *"Harness Your Entrepreneurial ADD:*

How to Move from Distraction to Action in the Age of Information Overload to Supercharge Your Profits." She is continually dedicated to discovering new ways to help people reach their true potential... creating success by design versus default!

CONTACT INFORMATION

Elisa Magill, MBA, Ph.D.
Endurance Business Builders
CEO, Brain Energy & Performance Expert
Endurance for Business, Endurance for Life!
(951) 426-0688
www.ElisaMagill.com
www.Linkedin.com/in/ElisaMagill

"

"Avoiding danger is no safer in the long run than outright exposure. The fearful are caught as often as the bold."

—Helen Keller

Ean Price Murphy

Dedication

I dedicate this chapter to Anna Forbes at Smooth Consulting.

Though I knew her briefly, she impacted me deeply.

30 Days to Financial Courage

by Ean Price Murphy

I was on a new client call this morning and she said, "I worry a lot about not having enough money. I guess I need to fix that mindset".

When did we get to the point where all our financial issues are seen as "mindset" issues?

Sure, there are money blocks most of us have, but that doesn't mean that having a healthy fear about not having enough is always a mindset issue. Or that not worrying about money at all is necessarily unhealthy. The question really is: are you living your financial life with ease or stress? Is your relationship to money healthy or full of dread? If you are one of the lucky few who have it all figured out, congratulations! But, if you are one who avoids thinking about finances, worries about money, or constantly has to adjust what you can afford because you have no proactive cash management system, there is a better way! One that doesn't have to mean tracking every penny in a multi-tab spreadsheet or obsessing over bookkeeping. A way that allows you to focus on the impact you want to have in the world and letting money help you fuel that impact.

When is worrying about money a mindset issue and when is it just needing to have a system?

Think of it as being lost in an unfamiliar place. Would you be mad at yourself for not knowing where you are? Would you try to ask for directions or would you say *"a map won't help because I can't even read a stupid map!"*

If you have thoughts like *"I could never earn that much"* or *"I'm not good with money or math,"* then those are mindset issues—judgments about your skills and abilities. Judgment and fear is rooted in history. Mistakes made by you or that you observed being made by others. But you are not doomed to make those same mistakes—you already have what you need to do better, and that is the willingness to be brave and make changes. By learning more, you can do better. For me, that is the definition of courage—feeling fear and being willing to take action anyway. You can learn the skills of financial literacy no matter what your money history has been.

I know this because well into my twenties, I was financially illiterate. I had grown up thinking that all I needed to know was

"Work Hard And You Will Succeed." But after working two, or sometimes three jobs for years, I found myself so far in debt from putting basic living expenses on my credit card that given what my income level was at the time, it would have taken me the rest of my life or longer to pay off the debt.

So, I filed for bankruptcy.

Ouch.

Filing for bankruptcy felt like a huge failure. Not only failure at being a proper adult and taking care of myself, but also failure to live up to my values of integrity and self-sufficiency. It took great courage to let that fear of failure go in order to move forward. I had to give up my current way of (not) dealing with my financial situation and build something new for myself.

Once I was able to face that fundamentally my problem was that I wasn't earning enough, that the quality of work I was doing deserved a stable living wage, and that no one was going to advocate for me better than I would, I could finally begin to take the right actions to fix my financial situation.

For me, that meant starting my own business so that I could determine my own income. I learned to ask for what I wanted and learned to say "no" to clients who didn't agree with the value that I provided. That was the mindset work I had to do. But, when it came to keeping enough of the money I was earning to be able to pay myself, my expenses, and my taxes—that was where I needed a system.

For many of us, fear around money stuff usually stems from two things: worry that no one will want what we have to offer and worry that we will be judged for our choices. In both cases, those fears are rooted in very real safety concerns.

If no one wants what I'm selling, I won't be able to make enough to live.

If those I rely on shun me for my choices, I will lose my community.

To me, those are safety concerns because the idea of self-sufficiency is B.S. We cannot, nor should we try, to do things on our own. We need the support of peers, mentors, and friends to be successful. If you don't have people in your life who lift you up and support you in being the best version of yourself that you can be, it is time to find some new sources of community, inspiration, and information to at least balance, if not replace, your current network.

Fear can strike at any level. You might have your financial house in order and be earning a great income but still feel like a fraud flying by the seat of your pants. Or maybe you aren't comfortable aspiring to the next level because that might feel too scary, or that you would be betraying your community to do so well.

Ironically, the only way to stop being afraid of something is to directly face the fear and take action despite the nerves. Nervous and exciting can feel very similar in your body, so celebrate knowing that if you are feeling nervous, something exciting and new is likely happening. Be willing to be a little uncomfortable. Make a plan to take small actions to challenge yourself in healthy ways where you know you will succeed, so that you can begin to gather evidence of your growing skills and strength. Stop, rest, and reward yourself as often as you need, no judgments. Remember that trying new things is stressful so be sure to be patient and gentle with yourself. Don't try to do too much at once. Big, dramatic efforts can feel good at the moment, but rarely affect real change like the slow and steady approach. Be sure to celebrate your progress, no matter how small, and to share your progress with others who will celebrate with you.

I like to think of getting financially literate like learning to drive a car. It can be scary at first, but if you make it a habit to practice safely, it soon becomes second nature. I learned to drive on my father's 1973 Volkswagen bug. It was a tiny yellow soda-can of a car, but sitting in the driver seat with buttons, levers, and pedals, I couldn't get over the feeling that if I did the wrong thing the car might explode, killing me, my dad, and everyone else on the road in a two-mile radius. Soon, with practice, I got comfortable. Comfortable enough to park on the hills of San Francisco with a stick shift and to fly down the highway, windows down, singing along to the radio. Well, as much as a 1973 Volkswagen can "fly." That car was lucky to get 45 mph on an uphill. And, even though now I was a comfortable driver, I never needed to bother with what was 'under the hood' (did you know VW bugs had their engines in the rear and storage under the hood?). I had a great mechanic to help me keep that machine running smoothly. In business, we have financial mechanics like bookkeepers, accountants, and advisors. So, remember you have done hard things before, you have learned all sorts of skills already, and with support, you can learn financial literacy, too.

So, where do you start?

Start by defining your short-term financial goals. Do you want to get out of debt? Bring home more money? Get a promotion?

Stop worrying about what other people think? Write down your ideas and pick no more than three things to work on in the next 30 days and find the person who is going to support you and hold you accountable. Pick something that you know you will be successful in doing, so if you want to pick only one thing that feels ridiculously small, great! Maybe it is just making one phone call or opening one bank statement. Once you have done it, you can always pick the next small thing to keep going, or you can stop, have a cookie, drink tea, take a nap, or whatever else recharges you. Remind yourself over and over *"I get things done when I allow myself to go at my own pace."* Think of it like confidence compound interest. It seems strange but if you do less you often get better results. My father would say *"slow is smooth and smooth is fast."* Whenever I'm about to do something new, I remind myself *"even if it doesn't work, no puppies were harmed."*

Allow yourself to feel the feelings. You might be frustrated, angry, worried, sad that you have to deal with this—that is ok. Take action anyway.

You might not naturally be a math whiz, but the good news is that you don't need to be. Money management involves shockingly little math. And, remember, even math skills are learnable.

It's ok to be a beginner and to ask for help. If you don't get a satisfying answer, keep asking. Ask *"Can you explain this to me?"* not *"I have a dumb question."* It is crucial that you feel listened to by your accountant and not talked down to. There is no reason to put up with condescension just because you think someone has more information than you do. There are so many wonderful brilliant people out there, go find the one that makes you feel great.

Use a personal money management app to help you track your money without obsessing over it. I like apps like YNAB that let me set budgets for categories I want to keep an eye on (maybe it is Dining Out or Shopping or Groceries that I feel like I can have the greatest amount of influence and impact over) and not have to worry about the rest of the ways I spend my money. I don't want to have to track every single thing, I just want to make sure I'm earning more than I'm spending, and remembering to set aside money for taxes, short-term savings, and long-term savings like retirement.

If you have a business, make sure you are using software designed for bookkeeping (not just excel or google spreadsheets!) and read the book, Profit First, by Mike Michalowicz to get the money management skills for your business.

You might consider hiring a bookkeeper to help you, but accounting is looking at the past and categorizing what has already happened when what most people need to know is *"what can I afford today?"* and *"am I ready for tomorrow?"* That is the very real fear my client was expressing in our first call together—*"how do I know if I'm ok or not?"* and that isn't bookkeeping or accounting. That proactive cash management is what Profit First Professionals such as myself specialize in. Most small business owners can do their own bookkeeping data entry until they have enough money and not enough time so it makes sense to outsource.

Once you have those systems and a supportive accountability network in place, it makes it much easier to challenge yourself to grow you and your business without feeling the fear of what you don't know, you don't know. No one will take better care of your future you, than you today, right now. Ask the universe for a bit of courage, go find your supporters, and begin to build that brave future you want.

About the Author

EAN PRICE MURPHY, the founder of Moxie Bookkeeping and Coaching Inc, teaches successful heart-driven entrepreneurs a dead-simple cash management system that works with their natural habits so they don't have to learn accounting to become permanently profitable and can focus on impact not spreadsheets.

Ean is a certified Mastery level Profit First Professional, Xero Platinum partner, Quickbooks ProAdvisor, and a certified business coach.

CONTACT INFO

Ean Murphy
Moxie Bookkeeping & Coaching Inc
ean@moxiebookkeeping.com
https://www.linkedin.com/in/eanpricemurphy/
www.moxiebookkeeping.com

"
"Above all, be the heroine of your life, not the victim."

– Nora Ephron

Gina Marie De Leon

Dedication

To my son Marco Ivan, my reason for waking up every morning and putting on my armor of courage to confront all challenges and opportunities that come my way.

30 Days to Experience Progress and Growth

LET'S FIND OUT

by Gina Marie De Leon

> **"**
> *"Courage is the first of human virtues because it makes all others possible"*
> —Aristotle

Many times, as I share my life story with others, the statement "you should write a book" often comes up. I've pondered on this for the last 10 years; however, something always stops me. Fear. Courage is defined as strength in the face of fear, pain, or grief. Why am I fearful of writing this chapter? Writing is not a strength of mine, I have never published before, followed by the gnawing question: what will people think of me? Courage answers, "Let's find out!!"

I hope my personal story will inspire women to understand that fear will always be a part of our lives, and if we choose to battle it, we'll become stronger and wiser the more we face it.

TRY SOMETHING NEW

> **"**
>
> *"Life is a matter of Choices, and every Choice you make makes you."*
> —John C. Maxwell

Six years ago, I lived in Mexico with my family, married for 19 years, and the mother of a 12-year-old boy. My husband provided a comfortable life for our family, and I was able to be a stay-at-home mom. When my son turned 9, I was ready to go back to work, but still wanted to be available for my family.

Have you found yourself at this crossroad?

One year later I was blessed with a teaching position and was also introduced to a secondary income opportunity as a part-time sales rep for a direct sales company. I had no experience in teaching or sales. However, I was ready to start earning my own money, which would provide the freedom to purchase something on my own without dipping into the family budget.

Are you open to new opportunities? No matter your age, education, or socio-economic background, new opportunities await you. Don't scoff at small opportunities, or menial tasks, these may take you to discover new hidden talents and understand your real purpose in life.

I continued teaching, and like most people who get involved with network marketing and don't understand the lucrative business it can be, I jumped from one Direct Sales company to another.

The unforeseen life circumstances of my husband being laid off, put me on a path to focus more on my second stream income. Within 4 months of focus and determination, I went from sales rep to team leader, and within a year, I was offered an opportunity that required me to move from Mexico to California to launch the US market. We needed the money, so as a family, we decided that I should accept the job offer. In January 2016, I moved to Los Angeles by myself with only twenty dollars in my pocket. I was not afraid, I was terrified!

Accepting this position also meant leaving my son behind in the care of his dad who continued to live in Mexico. Have you ever felt guilty for not being there for your children because work got in the way? Imagine your child is sick and you are living in another country. It's the most horrendous, awful, and empty feeling. It can crush you, but don't let it!

What got me through? My determination to provide for the family and be together soon.

Originally, the plan was to be reunited as a family within a year. In 2017, my husband chose to stay in Mexico and open his own business. Six months later, I developed breast cancer which required me to stay in California for medical treatment. This changed everything. It reminded me of an old Yiddish proverb, "We plan, God laughs."

Direct Sales opened an opportunity I never thought possible for a middle-aged woman, and it can do the same for you at whatever age.

WHY DIRECT SALES

> "
> *"Success in this industry is not in finding the right person, but in becoming the right person"*
> —Mike Dillard

Before sharing my passion for Direct sales, let me clarify a couple of things. Direct Sales is a business model where independent contractors (or representatives or distributors) sell a company's products and/or services directly to consumers. The difference is that in the MLM (multi-level marketers) or networking marketing business model, the independent contractors also make money from recruiting others to work for the company. Not all Direct Sales companies are MLM, but all MLM follow the business model.

Over a decade ago, I embarked on an exploratory journey in Direct Sales to supplement my income. What I found was so much more!

I reframed my way of thinking and took myself from living as a single mom with financial scarcity to a place of comfort. Allowing me to travel, to provide for my son's private education, while enjoying a flexible business lifestyle! I'm so very grateful for this journey, and now for the circumstances that brought me to look beyond my then bleak, day to day, circumstances. I see myself in the mirror now and thank God that my life is unrecognizable from 10 years ago!

I found my voice and passion to uplift women all around the world to begin their entrepreneurial journey in Direct Sales. It all began with the courage to get on a plane, fly to LA, learn new skills, many of which were self-taught by making mistakes, learning from those mistakes, and moving forward. I am not sharing new information here. How many times have you heard, "pick yourself up, and dust yourself off?" Who have you uttered these words to? Your kids, friends, colleagues; it's great advice so why don't we act on it ourselves?

COURAGE AND FEAR COEXIST

> **"**
> *"You gain strength, courage, and confidence by every experience in which you really stop to look at fear in the face"*
> —Eleanor Roosevelt

Courage is a choice, a learned quality, an acquirable skill, which can only be gained through practice. Courage is not the absence of fear, it's feeling the fear and acting anyway. If there is no fear, there is no need for courage. To destroy fear, you must battle with it regularly. The more you attack it, the weaker it gets.

Choose to become intrepid and battle challenges that come your way, and to become a role model for your family as they see a vibrant woman emerge through hard work and dedication of your newfound passion. The Direct Sales, Network Marketing, and MLM industries will expose your weaknesses as an entrepreneur, while at the same time providing a supportive environment where education and training are more readily available to help you skill up where you need to. It's a great way to get your feet wet as an entrepreneur. You will gain skills such as strategic planning, leadership, and public speaking, just to name a few. These skills will enhance all aspects of your life, and the best part is that you will become successful by helping others become successful. It's a win-win! I'm in awe of these courageous women who chose to do the work necessary to improve their lives both emotionally and financially. Many of them have become close friends, which is another huge plus in this business. You are never alone.

WHY SELF COACHING?

> **"**
>
> *"The greatest discovery of all time is that a person can change his future by merely changing his attitude"*
>
> —Oprah Winfrey

I've had the privilege to learn from many leaders in the field, and I want to give special thanks to my mentors Nicki and Grace Keohohou, co-founders of Direct Sales Women's Alliance, for sharing their passion in this field and introducing me to self-coaching*. It's a daily ritual which puts me in the correct gear for the day and ready to face the world!

When you choose to accept the challenge of self-coaching, it will help increase your success ratio by over 30%. Consistency is key, it must be done daily, and throughout the day. You may choose to keep a journal and jot things down as they come up, but if you recall at the beginning of this chapter, I mentioned I'm not much of a writer, so it took me a couple of months before I began keeping a journal. I'm much more interested in you experiencing how asking yourself the right questions can help you view your challenges differently. Ask yourself questions that will inspire you to begin your day, reflect and review in the afternoon, and close your day peacefully by reviewing and being grateful for all you accomplished during the day.

WHAT TO ASK?

> "
> *"Courage is the most important of the virtues because without courage you can't practice any other virtue consistently. You can practice any virtue erratically, but nothing consistently without courage"*
> —Maya Angelou

These questions are meant to empower you, not judge you. Appreciate, love, and be thankful for who you are.

First thing in the morning

- ❖ What am I most excited about today? What am I most proud of in my life?
- ❖ Whose life will I make a difference in today? What do I choose to accomplish today?

Throughout the day, after a call or event:

❖ How well did I engage the guests? What did I do or say that created results?

❖ What are 1 or 2 things I could have done differently? Who can I make smile today?

In the evening, reflect, review, close the day:

❖ What was the best thing about today? What areas of my life did I grow in?

❖ What or who am I grateful for? What am I looking forward to for tomorrow?

Remember the challenge is to assist us in consistently moving us forward, and not living in the past. Let's not waste time and energy in trying to fix what has passed, learn from the past, apply your learnings so you can continue to move forward to the future of your choice.

REFERENCES:

1. Self-Coaching, Raise your success ratio, by Direct Selling Women's Alliance & Elan Enterprises LLC.

2. Hero's Journey, a growth adventure in becoming a modern leader by Darren Hardy.

About the Author

GINA MARIE DE LEON, Founder of Direct Sales Blueprint, with over 10 years of field experience as a bi-lingual English and Spanish Direct Selling Leader, Trainer, and Coach. She's a proud partner of Powerful Women Today as a Mentor Expert, where she continues her love to teach and learn together as a tribe. Her passion for learning continues while pursuing her Certification as a Direct Sales Coach with Direct Sales Women's Alliance, and her ACC Coaching certification with ICF (International Coaching Federation).

She is passionate for an industry that opens the doors for culturally diverse women from different socio-economic, and educational backgrounds to become entrepreneurs. Her guiding compasses being God and Family.

It's my mission to empower multi-tasking women to accomplish greatness and reach new heights within this amazing industry. Guide them through the pitfalls of working from home to successfully integrate both their home and business lives to achieve success.

If you are new to Direct Sales or have been idling for a while in your home business, and are ready to scale up, and experience a flexible business lifestyle, let's connect on Linkedin: https://www.linkedin.com/in/direct-sales-blueprint-12223-gina-marie

Jackie Lapin

Dedication

To Jeff, Ken, Kelley, Felicia, Analisa, Lorenzo, Sara, Missi and Ann—who have made all things possible for the community of Changemakers we serve, and for me! With deepest gratitude!

30 Days to Your Big Stage

by Jackie Lapin

D o you imagine yourself on stage in front of adoring prospective clients, all rapt, listening to your empowering words, and then eager to join your community?

But there's a big gap from that image to where you are now?

- ❖ Maybe you're suffering from glossophobia (fear of speaking on stage)?
- ❖ Possibly you don't yet have a signature talk that you're confident about?
- ❖ Is it that you are reluctant to make an offer from stage because you fear rejection or believe that it will be too salezy?
- ❖ Perhaps you're just so wrapped up in your current business you don't have time to go find your stages?

These are all reasons that keep many women off the stages they deserve—and away from the audiences who need what they offer! Several of these reasons reflect a level of fear that holds women back!

But facing all these with courage will reward you with an infinite benefit that will not only sustain, but grow your business!

So how about we put you on a stair-step 30-day plan that will have you ready, willing, and able to get on that stage, and then finding and booking it!

DAYS 1-7: FEAR OF PUBLIC SPEAKING

Let's address that elephant in the room. You have something valuable to offer and you are doing a disservice to yourself and the people that need you by not delivering it into their hands.

Here are some ways to get over that fear so that you can begin confidently delivering your talk.

1. Reframe how you perceive speaking. If you are imagining that the audience is judging you—how you look, whether you are boring or inarticulate, or whatever is going on in your head—I have news for you. GET OVER IT! They don't give a darn about YOU! All they care about is whether you have valuable information that empowers them and changes their lives. So, instead, if you take the stage realizing that they NEED you, that what you have will help them and that you are in service to this crowd that is craving the wisdom

and resources you offer, then your butterflies will disappear. YOU ARE IN SERVICE TO THEM!

2. Here's a wonderful exercise that I credit to the brilliant speaker and transformational leader Barbara De Angelis: Before going on stage, imagine that the Universe/God/the force of Love is beaming down golden yellow light through your head into your heart. This is the information you are imparting to this crowd, filled with the light of illumination. See it extending from your heart directly into the heart of your audience members. Then see it leave their hearts through their heads and up into the heavens to improve the state of the world. You are speaking directly to their hearts. I always do this before going on stage as an implicit plea for my words to have the impact they need for the benefit of those in the audience.

3. Try some BOX breathing. Inhale and count to four. Hold that breath and count to four. Exhale and count to four. Stay still and count to four. Begin again. Do this 10 times. Focusing on your breath should calm you down.

4. Now, your next step is to go out and find a local audience, one that would be small and friendly and practice! Practice will build confidence and chase away those flutters and fears.

DAYS 7-14: YOUR SIGNATURE TALK

Your signature presentation must educate, inform, build rapport, solve a problem unique to this audience (your client avatar) and create an invitation that will take the participants to the next level. First and foremost, it must present valued information that will advance the audience's knowledge and expertise before it can offer any resource—be that a free or paid-product offer.

That is an important distinction. You need to have one presentation that enables you to make an offer of a paid product from the stage and a shorter one where you offer a free "lead magnet" that will attract the attendees into your opt-in list or that will induce them to have a strategy session (phone or zoom meeting) with you.

In your talk, you will want to tell as many stories as you can—whether they are your stories, your clients' case histories, or experiences that demonstrate the problem. Stories are what people recall...it's what impacts their emotions.

Here's a basic signature speech structure:

1. **START BY TELLING A STORY,** or engage the audience members by asking a question. This is the fastest and easiest

way to get your audience engaged. Raise your hand and invite them to respond by raising their hands when you ask a question.

2. **OFFER YOUR CREDENTIALS.** Somewhere in the presentation you will integrate validation of your expertise, why they should listen to you and respect what you are offering.

3. **DEFINE THE PROBLEM.** This is critical. You must make them feel the pain before you can present the solution.

4. **EXPLAIN WHAT THEY WILL LEARN.** Briefly tell them the take-aways that they will experience when paying attention.

5. **GIVE THEM YOUR ROAD-TO-SUCCESS STORY.** This is very important for rapport building and creating the confidence that you can show them the way to the promised land! Bring them along on your rags-to-riches personal journey.

6. **PRESENT YOUR TIPS**, the value-based content. This is where you show them a taste of what you know that can help them. It should leave them wanting more from you. Offer anywhere from three to five different strategies that move them forward. This should take a good 1/3 of your presentation, or a bit more.

7. **ASK IF THIS IS HELPFUL**, and indicate that there is a way to get more...to help them to their next step.

8. **PRESENT THE OFFER.** If a paid offer, this needs to include your full basic program and bonuses of products that help overcome the objections they might have when evaluating if this is essential for their lives or business. You need to paint a picture of what life will be like once they step into this new reality you are presenting. If your offer is a simple lead magnet, you can spell out its benefits.

9. **INVITE THEM TO INVEST IN THEIR OWN SUCCESS**, with you as their guide. (And we'll talk more about this next.)

10. **TELL THEM HOW THEY CAN ENROLL.** Give them a clear way to enroll—go to a webpage, hand out a form in the room that they can fill out, text to a number on their phone, etc.

If you would seek guidance on this, many speaker coaches can help you hone your presentation so that you are confident about its success and then work with you on your delivery.

DAYS 15-21: MAKING AN OFFER FROM THE STAGE

Yes, the word "sales" is a dirty word to many leaders. You immediately imagine a used car salesman or an overly aggressive marketer hawking "and there's more...!!" But let me provide a way to reframe this so you are approaching your offer differently.

Think of this as an invitation! You are simply inviting your prospective client to allow you to help them! They need what you have to offer. And you are extending a helping hand. You can give them a boost to the next level. So throughout your presentation, you can seed it by saying such things as "when I help my clients do this..." and "let me share with you how this has helped..."

So when you present this from the stage you are asking them if what they've just heard has been helpful...and would this also be of value....then you can reveal the next level – the invitation you are extending for them to invest in themselves.

Again, if you need more specifics on how to adapt the introduction of your products and resources either in a presentation or a strategy session, there are some great coaches who can support you on this...some are specialists in enrollment strategies and some are speaker coaches who include this in their repertoire.

Days 22-30: Where to Find and How to Book Your Stages

The last phase is where you actually begin looking for the right stages for your empowering presentation, and then outreach to get the booking.

First, you want to match your topic to meetings, venues, associations or events that are attended by your target audience. If you want to speak to women entrepreneurs, for instance, you'll want to speak at women's business networking meetings. If you are providing a resource to moms with autistic children, you'll want to talk at support groups for families with youngsters on the spectrum. Etc.

The next step is to google such meetings, either in your market where you can speak in person or over Zoom, if you want to stay close, or nationally, if you are interested in speaking virtually anywhere. Search on the resulting website for the contact person, their phone and email. You can use Meetup or Eventbrite to find these as well. However, if you really want to make this easy on yourself, go explore www.SpeakerTunity.com.

At SpeakerTunity, The Speaker & Leader Resource Company, the company has done all the research for you! You will find subscription services where you can get an array of North America speaking gigs for the transformational leader for minimal cost monthly. Or you can secure specific curated directories just for your local region with thousands of leads within driving distance (SpeakerTunity Cities®), or a directory of meetings, venues and associations across North America just in your NICHE where your target audience hangs out and you can speak virtually! (SpeakerTunity Speaker Specialties®) This is an enormous time saver! And a perfect solution if you dread the research! Shortly, SpeakerTunity® will also have conference finder service!

Next, once you've identified the contact person, you are going to want to send a proposal letter. It should be no more than 6 to 7 short paragraphs highlighting what you would like to speak on and why you would be a good fit for that booker's audience. You may also want to include a professionally-designed two-page Speaker One-Sheet to showcase you, your credentials, your results and your signature presentation. Again Speaker-Tunity® can help here. The company provides a Speaker One-Sheet design service, along with training programs on how to craft the perfect proposal letter and do the follow up to secure the booking.

So now that you have the letter and your Speaker One-Sheet, there is one last element to include and that is a short, 3 to 5 minute, video of you presenting. The best version of this is from a live in-person presentation, but if you haven't had that opportunity, a virtual presentation to a group can be edited for this purpose. Either way, it should be dynamic and show you at your best, engaging with the audience, presenting with verve!

What's next? Start sending those proposal letters!

And here's where that courage is required again. You may need to send a lot of letters, and do a ton of follow up to even get one gig! Bookers are bombarded with prospects and you have to hit the right booker, with the right need, at the right time. Sometimes that can take a while and you just have to have faith! Have the courage to keep it up, and then once you get one, you can leverage it to get the next one, by noting where you've just spoken before!

Make sure to post your successes on your social media and on your website. When you start accumulating gigs, build a speaker page on your website, include a short highlight video on the page, and add in your Speaker One-Sheet.

And don't forget to celebrate! Once you start getting booked, take a moment to breathe, reflect on your success and enjoy the momentum!

About the Author

JACKIE LAPIN is the Founder of SpeakerTunity, The Speaker & Leader Resource Company, providing leads, tools and strategies for leaders, coaches and entrepreneurs to get booked for speaking engagements, radio shows, podcasts, virtual summits, TEDx events and virtual networking. Explore 75 regional speaker lead directories, or leads just in your niche all across North America. SpeakerTunity is the Speaker's Ultimate Tool Box. www.SpeakerTunity.com.

CONTACT INFORMATION

Jackie Lapin
SpeakerTunity, The Speaker & Leader Resource Company
jackie@jackielapin.com
https://www.linkedin.com/in/jackielapin
https://www.facebook.com/jackielapin
www.SpeakerTunity.com

Jennifer Polansky

Dedication

I offer this up for the greatest good of all women. To the women who have come and gone, and those yet to be born. To the women who break themselves in order to get ahead, and to those who feel they aren't breaking themselves enough. You are seen, and you are loved. To the divine feminine present within all life. To the cycles that birth, create, bring forth ideas into manifestation, and also destroy and let die. May we heal the wounds that make us feel separate, and recognize the deepest desire we all share—to be loved.

May all women have the courage to love themselves exactly as they are, and feel the worthiness to manifest their dreams, in alignment with what's best for THEM and the future generations.

For all prayers spoken and unspoken. Aho.

The Courage to Love Yourself, Exactly as You Are

A PATH TO FREEDOM, PLEASURE AND INTIMATE LOVE

by Jennifer Polansky

I think the most courageous thing you can do is look deep inside yourself, and love and accept exactly what you find. Rather than trying to change it or distract yourself, having complete trust that everything is working out **for** you, and knowing that you both deserve and are worthy of that.

This is the story of my journey to uncover the innate self-love within me, which has allowed me the freedom to live life on my terms, have the courage to open up to true love with another, and how you can do that too.

Self-love is a lifelong, spiraling journey. As soon as you find a deep love and acceptance for one part of you, it opens to another layer just underneath that's been waiting for the light to touch it. Life is not linear, neither is our growth, and nor is that the goal, which is something I wish someone had told me from the beginning.

I believe the biggest challenge of our time is how disconnected we've become from our own true nature and rhythms. We live in a masculine driven, goal-oriented society, when our most innate human patterns are cyclical and feminine. Do you know what you're actually chasing or whose ideal you're hustling for? Money, power, and success are all substitutes for what humans truly desire at their core, which is to be loved. What we need now is a return to what really matters, so we can be healthier and happier, living by our own **natural** cycles, in reciprocity with a planet that is thriving **with** us, rather than being sucked dry for its resources. What we need now is a return to self-love.

The reason I'm able to support my clients in such a good way when it comes to feeling more joy, freedom, and self-acceptance, is because I've gone through it all myself. I've been my own test subject and continue to be. I go through all the waves that you do, and I let myself express them, sometimes even crumbling into a pile of tears on the floor. I allow myself to feel so fully because I trust in the cycles of nature, and have faith in my own. I also know that unless you explore and love the depths of your pain, you cannot know the fullness of your joy.

It's been a journey to get here, and I've learned to be grateful for it all, because before I reconnected to my true self, I lived my life based on how others said I should.

FOR SO LONG I WAS LIVING A LIFE I THOUGHT WOULD GET ME LOVE.

I did everything I was told to do in order to be successful, happy, and accepted by society. I pursued a career based on what others told me I was good at, and what I got praise and acknowledgement for. I expressed myself the way I thought men wanted so that I would be "chosen." I stressed and damaged my body to look the way society said was desirable and sexy. None of it was fulfilling, and in fact it drained me to complete burnout which took years to recover from. It wasn't until I finally stopped looking outside, and began the road inward, that I discovered an authentic life of pleasure, joy, and the courage to open up to divine love.

From the outside my life looked enviable. I was an actress living in New York traveling back and forth from LA, meeting interesting people with big claims. *"Yes!"* I thought. *"This is how I'm going to change the world. This is how I'm going to inspire people, and show them how powerful they truly are."*

Of course, though, it was an illusion. The whole entertainment industry is. Under my confident facade was a little girl who just wanted to be told she was good enough, and I would get stuck in thought loops for days worrying if I had sounded silly, or ways that audition could have been better. Even promises of success from directors and producers were mainly out of their desire to feel important. It was all ego driven and a distraction to what really mattered: authentic connection, and the knowing that we are worthy and enough, simply for existing.

THE ILLUSION FINALLY SHATTERED.

One day as I was walking through Manhattan, I looked up at a billboard and was met with a beautiful, flawless image of a woman's face. Her skin was smooth, clear, and I knew from experience that she'd spent hours in hair and make-up. At that moment I asked myself, *"Oh my gosh, is that really what I want? For little girls to look up at a perfect, photoshopped image of me and say, 'That's what I'm supposed to look like'?"* I saw how pursuing an acting career was only perpetuating the issue of why so many women and girls can't love themselves, and I couldn't stand to be part of the problem anymore. I wanted to be part of the solution. From that day on, one-by-one, I canceled my actor memberships and never went to a casting workshop again.

I turned down a film role because it was clear how misaligned it was, and I stepped forward into what would become my new career which, at the time, I had no model or map for.

At that point, I had been meditating for two years, practicing yoga and studying tantra. A year earlier I had nearly lost it in meditation when I recognized my entire career was essentially based on playing make-believe. Needless to say, I was primed for this final realization.

After so long being disconnected from myself and how to live life on **my** terms, the first step was to come back home to ME, learn who I truly was, and slowly retrieve the pieces of myself I'd given away in order to get love. As I learned to listen to my inner voice and stopped caring about other people's opinions, I forged my own path and formula for coming home to myself. Many of the tools I found guided me to look outward for the answers. The path I took led in. It also led me to my now fiancé, running a business that supports world-wide women's empowerment, and having the freedom to travel, spend months at a time in places like Costa Rica, and ultimately live a life I don't need a vacation from. The stories we tell are what make up our cages, and the key to living free is to reconnect with the inner world, let go of the stories, and honor the natural cycles within.

There are two things I wish someone had told me early on:

- ❖ We move in cycles, and the way I'm feeling from one day to the next is **always** going to shift.
- ❖ That's not only okay, it's NATURAL.

As human beings we are an extension of nature, which is cyclical, not linear. So many women I speak to think they need to *"put on a good face,"* which always shocks me. What this creates are superficial interactions and the belief that not happy = not okay, perpetuating the idea that we need to be happy ALL the time. The reality is that things aren't always great, and that needs to become normalized, embraced and celebrated. We need to know it's safe to show up authentically and that we'll still be loved even if we're sad, angry, frustrated, late, etc. In a world of polished online profiles, it's up to each of us to find the courage to love and accept ourselves, as this creates a ripple effect for women around the globe, and those to come.

Unless you are connected to your inner truth, self-love is like trying to hit a moving target. While it's clear that outside circumstances are always changing, what is more hidden (and less accepted) is the inner world. A woman's brain chemistry changes as her hormones do, which is literally every few days, and by about 25% every week! That means during ovulation you may feel motivated, patient, and social, which are easy qualities to love. However, about 5 to 7 days later, in your luteal phase, hormones have fluctuated and now you may feel more sensitive, closed off, and tired; qualities that aren't particularly prized by society. If you told someone you felt that way they might even try to "help" you get out of it or "fix" it. Cue self-loathing. If you really want to upgrade your life, connect with your feminine essence and cyclical nature, practice forgiveness and self-acceptance, and allow yourself to be exactly as you are. Keep reading and I'll show you how to do that in 30 days.

The first thing I'm going to invite you to do is connect with your womb. Yes, your womb. I promise that this connection will change everything. Even if you don't have a physical womb, the energetic imprint is always present.

PRACTICE THIS BASIC WOMB CONNECTION AT LEAST ONCE A DAY:

1. Take several deep breaths, inviting yourself into a calmed state. Inhale to fill your belly and lungs, exhale to relax your body from head to toe. Soften your belly.

2. Bring your palms together and rub them vigorously for 30 seconds to create heat.

3. Place your hands over your womb, feeling the heat radiate from your palms, and creating a connection.

4. Visualize your womb, and breathe into her. Ask questions like:

- ❖ How are you feeling?
- ❖ What do you need right now?
- ❖ How can I deepen my connection with myself?
- ❖ Do you have any messages for me?

The next step is getting intimate with your menstrual cycle. If you no longer bleed, you can consider the New Moon as Day 1 and follow from there, or see when in the month you naturally feel a dip in energy, and make that Day 1. It's simpler than you think, and takes very little time each day.

Day 1-3 of your menstrual cycle (or what I like to call "moon-time"), is the first few days that you bleed, and when you'll need the most rest. If you can allow yourself a full stop, you'll have more space to see what is authentically there for you. The best thing to do is simply "Be," and notice the places where you feel challenged.

PRACTICES DURING MOONTIME:

- ❖ Journal or meditate everyday about these questions:

» Where have I been pushing myself?

» How can I love, honor, and accept myself more?

» What ideas are within me that want to come forth and be created?

❖ Take a bath with epsom or sea salt and feel yourself cleansing limiting beliefs

❖ Do restorative yoga, or better yet, take a nap and do nothing

After a few days, as long as you've given yourself time to rest, the light will begin to shine in. Do your best to ease back into daily life. Imagine a butterfly that's newly emerged from its chrysalis. Listen to your body as your energy naturally rises toward ovulation (your inner Full Moon), and then gently descends again.

PRACTICES TO DO UNTIL ABOUT DAY 21 (OR A WEEK BEFORE YOUR NEXT MOONTIME):

❖ Journal or meditate everyday about these questions:

» In what ways can I express myself more authentically?

» What am I learning about myself?

» What is working in my life, and what isn't?

❖ Listen to, watch, or read motivational material

❖ Do cardio or take a Shakti Flow yoga class

Around day 21, or about a week before moontime, can become the most challenging time for women. It's when the darkest shadows arise, signifying emotions and issues that haven't been addressed throughout the previous cycle. The inner critic can get strong, bringing up self-doubt and questions around worthiness and enoughness. Remember this is a natural cycle, you are discovering the places within that need more love, and this too shall pass.

PRACTICES FOR THE WEEK LEADING UP TO MOONTIME:

❖ Journal or meditate everyday about these questions:

» What emotions are most present right now?

» What have I not said that wants to be expressed?

» What is rising to the surface to be witnessed, acknowledged and accepted?

» Where have I not been honest about what I need?

❖ Do chi gong or Yin yoga

The more you connect with your inner womb voice, and get to know your cycle, tracking your moods, emotions and thoughts, the more patterns you'll uncover and the easier it will become to accept them. This journey inward has given me the courage to follow my dreams, live life on my terms, and open my heart to authentic love with another (which has been another personal growth journey altogether!)

About the Author

Women's Transformation & Empowerment Mentor, Certified Nutritional Practitioner, Reiki Master Teacher, Womb Practitioner, EHF Facilitator, Yoga Teacher.

Using tantric and shamanic philosophy, with mindfulness and embodiment practices, Jennifer helps you become more conscious and empowered around the ways you've held yourself back. You'll uncover the root causes of repetitive patterns and limiting beliefs, learn how to transmute them, and develop more balance, pleasure and ease throughout your everyday life. This new perception and awareness, along with the tools you are given and the space held, creates a stronger foundation upon which to build the life you desire.

After working together, you'll feel more in tune with who you truly are, and deeply connected to the power and magnitude of your feminine essence. You'll experience a stronger sense of self-worth and enoughness, along with the confidence to use your authentic voice, and accept yourself exactly as you are.

The work Jennifer does comes out of her desire to see all women honor, love, and accept themselves as they are, and to live a life that's true to their hearts and higher Selves, for the good of ALL beings.

Jennifer provides private mentorship, runs retreats and classes, offers energy clearing & womb healing sessions, and creates opportunities to connect in sisterhood through online courses and programs.

You came here for a reason. The world needs you connected to that purpose now more than ever. The future generations depend on it. First find home within your body, connect with nature's rhythms, and lean into the safety and power of your divine feminine wisdom.

If you'd like extra support in coming home to your natural rhythms and authentic Self, to feel more joy, freedom and pleasure go to:
jenniferpolansky.ca or follow me on
Instagram @moderntantra.

Laurie Smith

Dedication

_____

I dedicate this chapter to my husband Kent Smith, my brother Jeffrey Slutzker, and my friend Trissie Manwiller, each of whom I will refer to at the beginning of my story. Thanks for helping me to get started, as I discovered my own path.

I want to thank Gretchen Apgar, who provided me with the special quote that I mention at the end of the chapter.

Finally, I must recognize the strong leaders with whom I currently work.

30 Days to Discover Your Inner Leader

by Laurie Smith

B eing a follower is much easier than being a leader, but it's also much less rewarding. I started out as a follower. I followed a friend to college. I'll just go there too! I followed a new boyfriend (now husband) to Europe. Sure, I'll travel to another continent with you, why not? I even followed my brother in relocating to Northern Virginia. He found a job for me. I was just going with the flow.

I don't think my mindset was unique. We can ask ourselves what we want out of life, but most of us start out in discovery mode. Taking random college courses and discovering my passion for a specific discipline is how I eventually found my way.

I began a career in human resources, not fully understanding everything that would be required of me. I soon learned that in this field, opportunities to step up as a leader would be presented early on. I was expected to solve other people's problems. I was required to facilitate training workshops. I had to make hiring decisions. Big stuff out of the gate.

The human resources field is currently dominated by women, including the head HR position. Most other executive level positions are held by men. Given this current reality, it's especially important for female leaders to support each other. My hope is that HR leaders are supporting and empowering other female leaders trying to break through the glass ceiling.

As this book is about empowering women, I'll start with how we can help empower other women as strong female leaders.

First, cheer them on. Promote their ideas. Look around. It won't be hard to identify female colleagues that you admire. Praise them and actively champion their work. Perhaps encourage them to speak up if they don't seem to be heard. If they're more junior than you, mentor them, or recommend them for bigger opportunities.

Second, create opportunities for women to grow and lead. Just as many schools offer women leadership programs, so can businesses of almost any type. There are even job sites designed from which to specifically recruit female leaders. Be creative and look for your own ways to support the effort.

Finally, if it has to be said, make sure you're leaving any pettiness where you left it, in middle school. Don't view another woman as a threat. Compliment her. Her ideas are good. Tell her this. Don't talk poorly to or about her. Find positive things to say behind her back. If she really irritates you, tell your family. Tell your journal.

Next, let's discuss how we can empower ourselves as strong female leaders.

First, if you've been cheering on other women, you'll likely be rewarded with some reciprocal praise. That's not why we do it and don't let this be the reason, but it doesn't hurt to have that little extra support. People notice when you are in their corner, and they'll want to join you in yours.

Second, don't allow others to talk over you and then complain that you're not being heard. If someone interrupts you, keep talking. Don't go quiet. Don't assume that what they have to say is more important, more valuable. I once worked with someone that would address rude behavior on the spot. They'd say, *"we can continue to discuss the topic at hand, but let's first address what just happened."* I love that approach, and have found it to be an effective practice.

Third, don't wait for opportunities to fall in your lap. Go after them. The gender pay disparagement is real, but don't let that stop you from negotiating for the salary or the position you deserve. Take chances. Be confident and bold. Are you waiting for permission? If so, I give you permission.

All this talk about leadership. So, why should we care about being a leader in the first place?

As I've learned, it's how we can make the biggest impact. It yields greater confidence and competence. It's how we grow, it's how we help, and give back to others. It's how we inspire and improve our environment and ourselves. I was fortunate to find a career that forced me to step up and lead, even if I was faking it until making it.

Your inner leader may be discovered as you serve your community – perhaps as a scout leader, a sports coach, or religious leader. Whatever the incentive, jumping in and tackling issues head on is the best way to learn.

The rest of this chapter focuses on ways to be a leader in the professional workplace. Within the next 30 days, action steps can be taken for each recommendation listed. Some of it is transferable to other areas of life, but as my focus has been more on becoming a leader in my field of work, I would like to provide practical examples of what has been working for me.

So, what will it require to be a leader in the professional arena?

It will require us to step outside of our comfort zones. Be seen. Not wait for an invitation. Here are some tools I've found that we can use to accomplish this.

NETWORK

This is easily the most important tool we have. Building and maintaining relationships is the biggest driver of a successful career. We're building and growing our reputation, getting to know other leaders in our field. Our network will serve us in so many ways, including sharing resources, invitations to conferences and events, and even cheering us on as we grow and succeed. I value my network as I do my close friends. In many cases, they're one and the same.

Over the next 30 days, I challenge you to connect with one new contact each day, preferably in a similar or related field. Introduce yourself, offer to share ideas, or to support them in some way.

LINKEDIN

LinkedIn is the #1 professional social media tool. Build a strong profile and be an active participant within your online community. Your profile should include a warm, engaging headshot and a short summary statement with a broad description of what you do.

The next step? Post! There are endless reasons to post, including company news, professional accomplishments or rewards, recognizing others professional accomplishments or milestones, promoting a conference or event, job openings and opportunities, or my favorite – funny workplace memes. Share others' posts, create your own, just get out there and mingle.

Over the next 30 days, I challenge you to post on LinkedIn at least once a week. The more you do it, the bigger your presence. That translates to leadership to me. Keep it positive and professional.

SPEAKING OPPORTUNITIES

This one is probably the scariest. I must admit that I don't actively search for speaking opportunities, however they find me anyway. I've been called upon to present to large groups. I've been required to facilitate training workshops for work, conduct open enrollment presentations, present via videoconferences to hundreds of employees (it's easier when you can't see your audience), and serve as a SME in a college classroom. The more you do it, the easier it is. People want you to succeed, so when presenting to large groups, keep that in mind. Create your talking points, practice, prepare for any and all possible questions, and just do it. I was once part of a group that provided feedback to employees learning how to improve their public speaking skills. Most common feedback included speaking in monotone, using filler words (um, like), and cluttering the screen with too many words and not enough images. Don't do those things. Instead, learn the content and material inside and out and share your excitement about whatever the topic. Most importantly, practice, practice, practice.

Over the next 30 days, I challenge you to find an opportunity to speak in front of an audience. Maybe it's a small audience that just involves presenting an idea to your team or a social club, or a large audience that involves presenting a slide deck to the entire company. If this is still too far of a reach, perhaps sign-up for a public speaking course online or ask your supervisor or HR department for ideas to help you grow in this area.

TRAINING

It's easy to complain that our companies aren't training us on leadership, but we need to recognize that a natural leader will seek out training opportunities for themselves.

For online leadership training opportunities, there are many helpful, low-cost resources. LinkedIn Learning offers an endless number of leadership courses. Coursera is another good tool, often with free online courses.

For in-person leadership training opportunities, there are volunteer opportunities everywhere. Perhaps a local membership association or special interest groups. Check out Idealist's job board at www.idealist.org, currently listing over 5,000 volunteer opportunities. There must be a leadership opportunity for anyone with that number of listings.

In my case, most recently, I led a monthly discussion group on various HR topics with my local SHRM chapter. I selected the guest speakers, chose the location, and announced the events. I was ultimately responsible for all aspects of the meetings. Every month for three years, unpaid.

Over the next 30 days, I challenge you to enroll in a leadership course, or find a volunteer opportunity which will allow you to practice your leadership skills.

SERVE ON A BOARD

Serving on a board is a great way to discover your inner leader. Many working boards are in need of help, even those who are junior in their careers, to help carry the workload. The work is primarily completed outside of regular work hours, and will serve as a great opportunity to learn, get noticed, network, and build your resume. What are some roles that are needed? Perhaps providing social media support, or treasury support, or even simply taking minutes at meetings.

Over the next 30 days, I challenge you to identify a group to join that may eventually lead to an opportunity such as serving on their Board. Start small here and don't commit to anything until you've spent time getting to know the group. Becoming a member is a great place to start.

MENTORSHIP

If you currently have a mentor, you are one of the fortunate ones. Many universities now offer formal mentorship programs for both students and alumni. Take advantage of this if you can. If that's not an option for you, look around at all the other places you can find a mentor.

Over the next 30 days, I challenge you to reach out to a prospective mentor on LinkedIn, seek out someone from a conference you attend, or even ask a well-respected colleague to refer someone for you. It might take some effort, but if this works, it could be worth-while. Just make sure to be respectful and considerate of other people's time.

If you have a few years under your belt, this is your opportunity to give back. During the Obama Administration, I was consulting for the National Mentoring Partnership. The keynote speaker for the 2011 annual conference was Michelle Obama. To quote her, *"We should always have three friends in our lives—one who walks ahead who we look up to and follow; one who walks beside us, who is with us every step of our journeys; and then, one who we reach back for and we bring along after we've cleared the way."* Over the past decade, her quote has stuck with me.

The list of opportunities to explore are endless. There are still a few on my list, such as becoming a published author, starting a podcast, and obtaining an executive coach. I could go on.

While we explore our opportunities, it's imperative we remain cognizant of the leadership behaviors we're demonstrating. This is at the forefront of it all. We need to be the type of leader we expect of others. Trusting and trust-worthy. Giving credit to others. Leading by example. Putting people first.

"

"A sign of a good leader is not how many followers you have, but how many leaders you create"
—Mahatma Gandhi

About the Author

LAURIE SMITH has spent more than 20 years practicing HR. She received a Master of Science in Business degree from Johns Hopkins University, and a Bachelor of Science degree from the University of Baltimore. She is SPHR certified from the Human Resources Certification Institute (HRCI) and served on the Board of Directors with Dulles SHRM, where she spent years leading discussion groups on various HR topics.

CONTACT INFORMATION

Laurie Smith
lauriesmith717@gmail.com
https://www.linkedin.com/in/lauriesmithsphr/

"
"She is clothed with strength and dignity, and she laughs without fear of the future."
—Proverbs 31:25

Leona Krasner

Dedication

To my mama, who taught me to be limitless.

Courage in Relationships

DISCUSSING THE TOPICS OF GROWTH, TRANSFORMATION, EXIT COURAGE AND RELATIONSHIPS, AT EACH STAGE

by Leona Krasner

Courage is not the first word that comes to mind when considering relationships. Nevertheless, it can be a little scary to take a stand for your positions closer to the start of a relationship, knowing that doing so may spell the end of something exciting and new. It can feel even scarier to rock the boat, especially when you've got a mostly good thing going, by trying to change the status quo. Scariest of all can be the prospect of ripping apart a longer-standing relationship with someone you know so well, including their good, bad, and ugly. This chapter will not only explain precisely what to look out for if you're looking for some courage in any of these regards, but will also give you a step-by-step action plan for what to do if you find yourself in one of these buckets.

Relationships sometimes seem to come with a sort of finality, no matter where you are in the relationship. There is single-ness, which is often portrayed as, and may often even feel, lonely and to-be-avoided. Finding someone, almost anyone, really, can sometimes feel like a level-up over this dreaded singleness.

We also often hear about this idea of sacrificing for the other. Sucking it up. Putting up with the bad and enjoying the good for the sake of the other, or family, or God. I've got news for you though. You happen to be in the driver's seat of your relationship, and have far more control over the direction in which your relationship goes than you may know. And talking about what is critical for you at the start of a relationship, or what is not going well during a relationship, or getting out of a relationship that is truly not good for you, are all doable, achievable things that we will discuss step-by-step in the pages ahead.

Years ago, I found myself tiptoeing a bit, mentally, at the start of any relationship that seemed to have potential. My goal was to put my best self forward, to show this person the best version of myself, and to not be too nitpicky, lest I push the other person away. As a result, I often attracted, and accidentally managed to retain the attention and affections of exactly the wrong men, who were definitely not my ever-afters. The more I was true to myself, however, and specifically not only focused on my must-have characteristics and deal-breakers, and more importantly, shared these with the other person, the more successful my relationships became. I encourage you, if you are single or are casually dating, to begin thinking about what your must-haves and deal-breakers are.

Once you're in a relationship for a while, and it seems to be working, I can attest to the serious cojones it can take to open your mouth and spew displeasure – or, at least, so it has felt in some of my prior relationships. In fact, your relationship is constantly growing. You two are always getting just a little bit closer or a little bit farther apart emotionally. We will delve into the specifics of what to say and how to say it a bit later in this chapter, but for now, if you're in a longer-term relationship, what really grinds your gears about your partner? Try to think more about specific behaviors instead of innate characteristics. You two will be able to work on the former, but only your partner might be able to work on the latter, and only if they are personally inspired to do so.

Are you in a long-term relationship that makes you feel more bad than good? Where you feel down more often than you feel great? Where you feel as though you have to walk on eggshells, constantly waiting for the other shoe to drop? Been there. It sucks. The thought of having nothing, being alone, and having zero good times instead of just occasional good times current-ly, can often feel even scarier. There's a better way, but it will take courage. Get out a piece of paper, and make a list of what you are putting up with in a person, and what your absolute must-haves are for your next person. Enough settling. We're going to discuss not only your exit plan, but how to narrow your scope so you're crystal clear on exactly who you'd like to meet, and with whom you will never settle again.

One big area that often gets neglected, to the couples' detri-ment, is discussing and making a plan around finances. A pre-nuptial agreement, whether you two even need one, and what one might include, is an important part of the talk about financ-es, especially if you, your partner, or you both are coming into this relationship with a career, money, a potential inheritance, a business, or a trust. Turn the four-year-old, curious little person switch on your head when you discuss these topics.

YOUR COURAGE PLAN TO STARTING A RELATIONSHIP ON YOUR TERMS

New relationships are exciting! If you two get to a second date, it likely means that the other person was, hopefully, at minimum cute, interesting, and not nuts enough to warrant a second date. You are on the path! Let's talk about planning the path a bit, instead of taking the random twists and turns that have likely frequently abounded at the start of previous relationships.

Have you ever felt as though you were attracting the precisely wrong kind of person to you? For me, especially when I was in high school and college, it seemed as though guys who were bursting to be helped with their myriad of issues were everywhere. Turns out, there are plenty of other guys out there, but I needed to go at this process a little more actively before I could begin meeting the right sorts of people with whom I could actually envision building a life together. Let's talk through the steps.

First, make a list of must-have attributes of your forever person. This isn't the tumble in the hay person, or the rebound person, or sometimes person if you're lonely. This is the person with whom you're serious about having a long-term future. What is absolutely essential for them to have, characteristic-wise? Think in terms of the following categories: looks, career, goals, interests, outlook on life, outlook on family, and passions, just to name a few. Consider what you didn't like about past exes. We are not thinking about behaviors in this portion, but innate features. For me, I was looking for someone family-oriented, driven, governed by a moral compass, passionate about helping others, giving, adventurous, affectionate, and willing to be silly.

Next, make a list of absolute deal-breakers. Deal-breakers are those characteristics that you refuse to put up with in a partner. Not the little things that you can overlook, but those traits that are big enough to make you go, never again. Even if the person is the absolute best in every other way, having just one of these means that the relationship simply cannot work. For me, deal-breakers include mooching off me, arrogance, treating me as lesser, lack of ambition, unreasonable competitiveness with me, using me as either a physical or emotional punching bag, pulling me down instead of lifting me up, greed, stinginess, and lack of commitment.

Now comes the hardest part. Often in life we put up with the bad until we literally cannot anymore. We stay in the job where we feel overworked, underappreciated, and definitely underpaid, until we finally have enough. When that moment comes, it's as though a switch has been thrown, and we're able to make the decision we had been avoiding and putting off, sometimes for years, with no difficulty at all. I challenge you to be brave and to say enough to the losers, to those people who put you second. Those who made you feel underappreciated, not enough, and just bad. It's time to focus on the right fit, those who make you feel incredible. But that means we need to throw the switch to only continue to go on dates with men who meet the criteria on your must-have list and don't have any of the items on your deal-breaker list. Yes, that means letting go of the really hot person from last Tuesday who was maybe kind of dismissive to the wait staff, and also to you, during your date. It means no longer wasting your time with the wrong people. It means specifically selecting who you want to see again. And yes, it does mean going against the flow of just saying yes to that next date. I am asking you to be courageous, right now, and resolve to only date the people who fit your list.

How to do this? It means getting to the juicy, getting to know you, questions on the earlier side, perhaps as soon as dates two or three. It means keeping your eyes open to the other person's words and behaviors and, even more importantly, the ones they don't say or demonstrate, from day one. This person might be your partner for a very long time, and it's up to you to do your due diligence in a comfortable, conversational way that's simply part of your date. You get to set the tone. So, ask them what inspires them, and be ready to share with them what inspires you. Do they want kids? You don't want to only discover the answer to this question two years from now, and realize that it absolutely doesn't match your answer. What do they want to be when they grow up? Be brave, put that detective hat on, and be ready to share your own answers, openly and honestly, too.

YOUR COURAGE PLAN TO TRANSFORMING YOUR RELATIONSHIP ON YOUR TERMS

So, you two have been dating for some time, and you think this one might be the one, but there are just a few things... I hear you. Fortunately, you have the ability to steer this relationship in a better direction, but it'll take your initiative. Here's the thing. The relationship will not change unless you do something about it. Let's discuss the steps to help your relationship thrive.

First, consult with the list of behaviors that you would like your partner to change. I remember the roommate feeling that constantly splitting every single check with an old boyfriend felt like. Ironically, I was likely the one who had initially offered to split the very first check way back at the beginning, and I felt as though I had to keep offering every time after that. Hated it. What are some behaviors that your partner showcases that just rub you the wrong way? Some behaviors that had previously rubbed me the wrong way included: prioritizing his interests over me even when I asked him to stop, fixating on what I did wrong instead of what I did right, leaving me alone at parties for almost the entire night, lack of excitement when I came home, constantly comparing themselves to me, never wanting to talk on the phone, immediately getting up from the dinner table as soon as they were done eating instead of waiting for me to finish, and keeping the toilet seat up.

Next, prioritize your list. Some of the behaviors will likely hurt way more than others. Put the most painful behaviors at the top of your list. Then, think about how you would like for your partner to concretely change their behaviors so that their new behavior works better for you. What, specifically, should they start or stop doing? Be very careful here – we are not looking to attack or change the person's personality or characteristics, just behaviors. For instance, regarding the time that an ex would prioritize his interests over me, I realized that what I really wanted was scheduled "us time," where we focused attention on one another. By thinking of ways to fix the behavior, instead of just fixating on the hurt feelings, I activated the logic centers of my brain, and it became easier to frame the conversation with my partner when the time came.

Finally, ask your partner if they would be open to scheduling a specific time each week when you two will discuss the awesome parts of your relationship and what could be going better.

Don't spring this on them when they're stressed or tired or anxious or hungry. Instead, casually bring it up when you two are feeling calm and happy. Then, once they agree, it is your job to ensure that you two actually have the talk when you said you two would.

Short-term, it might feel a little weird and a lot vulnerable to open up about things that your partner has been doing that hurt you. But keep pushing, keep sharing those specific instances that they did – or didn't – do something, and resolve to make a plan together about how you two can make things work better for you going forward. Then, extend them the same courtesy, and ready yourself, first, to listen, and second, to be open to changing your ways. This is not a one-way street. They can't be the only ones doing the changing.

YOUR COURAGE PLAN TO SAY ENOUGH

Why do we put up with bad? As in, pretty bad, really bad, in fact. Crying yourself to bed more nights than not. Pain – emotional or physical. Hurting and feeling as though you aren't enough. But the alternative – loneliness – often feels even scarier, until there is just no other option.

I need you to write down what your idea of the perfect life, and perfect partner, was before you met your current person. What was most important to you then? What is most important to you now? What will you absolutely need in your next relationship, taking particular note of the things that you were putting up with that were hurting you so deeply in your current relationship? And what will you no longer, never again put up with? Really dig deep. Feel the feelings, but write this list.

Next, I need you to decide for yourself whether you will allow yourself, in good conscience, to keep putting up with a relationship that is hurting you so much, or whether enough is enough. What will you be shedding if you go? What will you no longer have to put up with? What will you now have the opportunity to do?

Most important, if you are in any danger, get help. Call 911. Get that restraining order. And that restraining order can be for something as seemingly small as your partner continuing to call or text you nonstop after you ask them to stop. You deserve better. I give you permission to leave.

About the Author

LEONA S. KRASNER, Esq., MBA, first became interested in relationships and justice at the age of seven, when she decided to become an attorney. As she studied the Social Sciences, her major at Brooklyn Technical High School, and then went on to double major in Psychology and Politics at New York University, her interest in relationships and justice only grew. Her studies at Washington and Lee University School of Law, where she earned her Juris Doctorate, and then at the Stern School of Business at New York University, where she earned her Master's of Business Administration, shaped her decision to pursue the law, and then start her own law firm. Today, Leona is the Managing Partner of Krasner Law, PLLC, a family law firm that helps folks in New York and New Jersey get married, stop being married, and help with the children, too. Her boutique law firm is quickly expanding, and she currently has twelve employees. When not assisting clients with their family law issues, Leona regularly posts relationship tips across social media. Her ideology is that she would love to help people strengthen their relationships, if at all possible. If that doesn't work, she and her firm stand ready to assist.

When not practicing law, Leona helps students as Managing Director of Krasner Review, LLC, a tutoring company that assists students with standardized examination preparation, application preparation, and scholarship negotiation. She also enjoys managing and performing at concerts that she puts on as Managing Director of her nonprofit organization, Tunes for Tots & Teens, through which volunteer musicians play concerts for children. She also enjoys going on adventures with her husband, traveling, and reading.

CONTACT INFORMATION

Leona S. Krasner
Krasner Law, PLLC
Leona@lkrasner.com
www.lkrasner.com
https://www.linkedin.com/in/leonakrasner/

Lil Barcaski

Dedication

Everything I do, everything I write, everything I am is for the two most important people in my life. You guys know who you are. I love you both more than everything.

Writing for the Greater Good

by Lil Barcaski

I am a ghostwriter. No, that does not mean that I write stories about ghosts (although I do write a young adult fiction series about a girl who talks to them.)

I write for other people whose name is typically listed as the author on the book cover or article though they most likely didn't write a single word. When people ask me if it bothers me when I see someone else's name as the author on a book I wrote, my answer is always the same. *"Not when I go to the bank."*

Ghostwriting pays well, and I appreciate that, but that's not the only reason I chose this career. The best thing about what I do is that I get to tell stories. In fact, I get to help other people tell their stories.

I write all kinds of things, business books and blog articles, and I've even written some fiction that was surprisingly well received, but my favorite thing to write are memoirs. I've written some doozies. I have had a front row seat to the lifetime movie of some incredibly courageous people, mostly women. Knowing what some of my clients have survived and are willing to share with the world astounds me. To be trusted to write their stories for and with them is a gift not many people are given.

They humble me.

WHAT EXACTLY IS COURAGE?

I am also a playwright and I have been blessed to watch actors tread the boards saying the words I wrote. It's a fun, yet a nail-biting, experience to sit in the audience among the theater goers who are watching your play, praying they will laugh in the right places, moved when you look over to see a grown man crying over your words being performed. It's scary, but it's a rush.

Courage is a relative term. I am painfully shy by nature, a fact that floors most people who know me because I am very good at presenting myself as outgoing. Excellent acting training has made that possible. I highly recommend taking an improv or acting class if you too are afflicted with the shy gene.

Books have always been a great place to hide for me. Movies too. I worship film, especially old film, black and white, grainy, and beautiful. I love the clothes, the cars, the over-the-top drama of the actors of the 30's, 40's and 50's. They are story driven works of art. I could immerse myself in movies, sit in a dark theater, with a popcorn bucket perched precariously on my knee every day of the week.

However, I have bills to pay, a company to run. I have people who need me. So, I push myself out the door, or nowadays, onto my Zooms, and into interviews on podcasts and summits to talk about writing, publishing, and marketing books. I tell funny, and sometimes not so funny stories. I make jokes to hide my nervous, anxiety ridden nature. And somehow... I pull it off.

Is that courage? Maybe. It's not the courage I had as a kid to surf the waves of the Jersey shore or ride my Yamaha 250 motocross bike across the marshes of the meadowlands. It's not the courage I had to play music in front of hundreds of people.

I've done what a lot of people would consider courageous things most of my life. I've taken the leaps into new careers, new places to live, crazy adventures. I have always believed in the adage – Jump and the net will appear.

It always has. I believe it always will.

COURAGE TAKES YOU PLACES YOU MIGHT NOT OTHERWISE GO.

Today, I live and work in a 35-foot Class A motorhome. I drove this giant hunk of tin from Florida to Utah, through the southern states, up through Texas, down through Arizona and New Mexico and back. I went over 7000 miles, drove the Loveland Pass out of Denver in the dark, only to realize I had never checked to see if the headlights worked (not so much). I went over mountains, drove through horrible rain and wind, on crappy roads with construction going on, over giant overpasses. Did I mention my debilitating fear of heights?

But here's the thing. I got to see the arches of Moab, the snow-capped mountains of Colorado, Monument Valley, the giant windmills in Texas that look like they are walking steadfastly across the plains, a trick your mind plays on you.

There are things we all want to do, things we may not have the courage to attempt. There are stories we want to share but are afraid we will be judged by others if we share them. Afraid of who we might hurt. Worried that we aren't good enough or have enough to say.

❖ What if I write a book and no one buys it?

- ❖ What if I write my story and no one thinks it was worth telling?

- ❖ What if I start my book but never find the courage to finish it?

Will that make me a failure?

What if I start a business and no one buys what I'm offering? What if...?

THE PARADOX OF THE HUMAN CONDITION, ACCORDING TO LIL:

"

We are all desperate to be seen.
... and we are all PETRIFIED to be seen.

When it comes to the fear of being seen through your writing, even if you're writing a business book, you have stories to tell. And they are more interesting than you think. People may not find your book about your best sales techniques riveting, but I promise you that if you tell them stories about how someone you taught to be a great salesman became a top producer, how you affected his or her life, what that person did with your awesome training, that's interesting. I like to call these business memoirs.

Whatever it is you do, be it coaching, consulting, sales, marketing, manufacturing, financial planning, real estate... tell your story. Tell the stories of the people you've helped, learned from, those who changed your life, your mindset, your heart.

More importantly, find the courage to share the times you failed, the losses, disappointments, and trials. Seeing that you have made it through those difficult waves (once a surfer, always a surfer) will help other people find the courage to take action.

You won't have to worry that no one will buy your book. You will have built a platform to speak from, a place to start to share your information and expertise, guidance, and wisdom. That sells books. That sells YOU.

If you're writing a memoir or a biography, have the courage to tell the truth. Share things that will help other people learn and grow. Show them that it's possible to start or grow a business even if you fail a few times, to get through a difficult divorce or the loss of a loved one, to suffer severe health problems and recover, or face the challenge of changing careers later in life.

WHY THE GREATER GOOD?

This year, I am committed to the concept of writing for the "Greater Good." This book is doing just that and I'm proud to be among this distinguished and caring group of professionals. The authors in this book are sharing their expertise, their techniques, their stories about courage.

We are all committed to giving you action items that you can implement week by week to raise your bar on courage, take your business to the next level, change your attitude toward positivity, gratitude, and prosperity.

I promise you that if you write anything, a book, blogs, a chapter in an anthology, even social media posts, and you write from the perspective of how what you are sharing will help others, you will succeed. You will be thinking of the greater good, not just showing off or trying to make a sale or gain a new client.

If you approach writing, business, sales, coaching, even life from that point of view, you will be seen as a person with integrity. You will make more sales, get more clients, I promise.

NEVER LET FAILURE GET IN THE WAY OF A GOOD TIME.

Lots of people are afraid to write and even more afraid of public speaking. Many people are afraid to ask for money, or at least the amount of money they are worth. Women especially are often afraid to ask for a raise or apply for a job they're worried they might not be 100% qualified for. Did you know that men apply for jobs they feel they are, on average, about 70% qualified for, whereas women will not apply for the same job unless they meet every single criteria listed?

Mostly, like I said, we are petrified to be seen. We are all afraid of failure.

Truth is, failure is just the kissing cousin of courage.

Whether you want to find the courage to write a book, start a new business venture, leave a bad marriage or relationship, ask for a raise or raise your rates, move to a new city or... become a digital nomad in a 35-foot Winnebago, it starts with knowing what it is that's stopping you.

Here is a set of exercises you can do to effect some change in your life and find the courage you need that can make a difference in 30 days – like we promised when you opened this book.

Week 1:

List 3 things that you would like to accomplish or something you are afraid to do that you would love to tackle.

Examples:

- ❖ Raise your rates for coaching or consulting
- ❖ Write and submit an article to an online magazine
- ❖ Fire a client that is taking up too much of your time and energy
- ❖ Apply to speak on a summit

It could be something personal like:

- ❖ Having a difficult conversation with a friend or loved one.
- ❖ Sharing a story about a traumatic experience

Or something fun but challenging that you always wanted to do like:

- ❖ Getting up and singing at karaoke night
- ❖ Skydiving or windsurfing

Make two columns: one with the pros and one with the cons of making these a reality.

EXAMPLE:

If you want to raise your rates, what will happen when you an-
nounce that new rate to a new potential client? What will your
existing clients say when you let them know your rates are going up?

Will you lose the job to someone cheaper? Lose the client
you've given great value to for a long time?

Or...

Will you make the money you deserve? Will you realize you are
worth more than you've been asking for and start to get it?

Week 2:

Pick one thing from the list and begin to implement a plan to
make it happen. Test things out on a friend or family member.
Ask them to listen to your idea for a story. Practice a sales call
where you tell the potential client that your bill rate is 25% higher than you have been charging up to now.

Choose your "money song" and practice it in the shower.

Call the skydiving place!

Week 3:

Be courageous for 10 seconds at a time. By that I mean, when you find yourself panicking about this thing you have decided to try, that you need or have the burning desire to do, allow yourself to think about that thing. See yourself doing this courageous act. Picture it in your head, and for 10 seconds let the bravery wash over you. Push the fear aside and just breathe.

Rinse and repeat.

Week 4:

Be brave and do the thing you chose week 2. Jump. Don't look down, just believe in the net. Ask for the raise. Submit the article.

Strap on the parachute.

Remember the cowardly lion? When the time came, he was the most courageous of all. He is all of us. We just don't know it until the moment comes when we have to be the lion.

About the Author

LIL BARCASKI has been a self-starting entrepreneur for her entire 30 plus year career. She has a diverse background from owning and operating successful restaurants and catering companies to being a highly trained writer and performer.

For the last 15 years, Lil has been a much sought-after ghostwriter. She has ghostwritten dozens of books in the business, memoir, and even fiction genres, and has authored many of her own books, plays, and screenplays.

Lil also trained in acting, directing, and stagecraft in her home state, New Jersey, and later at New York University (NYU). She is a S.A.G. actor and an accomplished and highly trained drummer and vocalist. She uses her training in acting when coaching burgeoning speakers.

Lil believes in working and writing for The Greater Good. When you write and work to inspire, educate, and elevate others, you are living your best life with integrity and honor.

CONTACT INFORMATION

If you ever want to talk about writing your story, here is how to connect with me.

Lil Barcaski

CEO Ghostwriter's Network

Business Strategist – Ghostwriter/ Publisher – Speaking Coach – Playwright
www.ghostwritersnetwork.com
https://www.linkedin.com/in/lil-barcaski-957b5323/
https://www.facebook.com/GWNPublishing

Marianne Bjelke

Dedication

Quinn,

For all the times you thought me strong

I must confess, you helped me without being aware.

Courage is sometimes easier to find in ourselves

when we want to be strong for others.

You are my inspiration

and my "Why."

I love you to the moon and back.

Always.

Unmute Yourself

DON'T LET THE FEAR OF PUBLIC SPEAKING KEEP YOU SILENT

by Marianne Bjelke

The drumming in my ears and the echo of my breath surround my head like a fog I can't escape. I make my way slowly, grasping for purchase and afraid to look down, lest my fear of open heights paralyze me completely.

Holding my breath as my fingertips search for any handhold, I take small careful steps and try not to lose my balance. It's just another 20 feet (pointing) over there. And I just need to get there without falling off the edge.

Because this is not how it ends for me. Not today. My seat is just RIGHT over there. I can make it.

Part of me knows with certainty that this theater balcony will NOT come crashing down under my weight as I slowly make my way over there, holding on white-knuckled to the back of each seat I pass. Yet my body still feels all the symptoms of terror in a very real way.

The likelihood of losing my balance to trip comedically over three rows of empty seats and sail helplessly over the balcony banister to land 20 feet below on the ground floor (where, for the record, it would be MUCH SAFER TO BE SITTING)... well, the odds of any of that happening are low. I get that.

But that's my fear. It's my Achilles heel that I offer up to you as Exhibit A. The fact that it's irrational doesn't make it any less real at this moment.

Maybe you think it's silly to have such anxiety over something so safe and simple as walking through the open space of balcony seating. As you settle in to sit next to me, I admit now that the experience is behind me, I feel a little silly too. What was I so worried about? Why did my heart rate increase, my breathing become labored, and my body shake, all because I was in this awkward but certainly not life-threatening situation?

The lights dim slightly as the keynote speaker is introduced. They come out on stage with poise and confidence that emanates so strongly, we can feel it up here in the "cheap seats." Within a few minutes, they make us laugh. Throughout their presentation, they ask questions that make us think about how we can apply their topic to enrich our own lives. They fold in statistics and real-world facts with stories from their own life to connect with us as they teach us something new. There are hundreds of people here, and yet we feel like they are speaking directly and only to us.

That's when you lean over to me and say, "I could never do that. I'd be terrified."

Facing your fear is the only way to exhibit courage. There is no bravery without first being afraid.

You may have heard that more people fear public speaking than fear death. According to Psychology Today, fear of public speaking is rooted in the idea that you will humiliate yourself in front of an audience. What if you tripped or made a mistake? What if no one resonates with your topic?

I have good news for you. It's normal for experienced and novice speakers alike to feel some anxiety before going on stage (whether virtual or live). The difference is that experienced speakers have techniques to help them deal with and overcome the physical manifestations of nervousness.

Do you want to get over your fear of public speaking?

I've got good news for you. Confident and effective public speaking may seem a lofty goal, but you are up to the challenge.

1. **Write your speech about what you know best.** Sharing your personal stories and anecdotes that help you reinforce and share your expertise has many benefits. It establishes your credibility, connects with the audience, and sets you apart from the pack. No one is better suited to tell your stories than you are.

2. **Research to reinforce your point.** Familiarize yourself with the topic you'll be speaking about. Are there any current events you can refer to that will keep the audience engaged? Are there any facts or statistics you can include that reinforce the points you want to share with the audience?

3. **Love your audience.** It's natural to worry about what the audience will think of you. This is where the fear can start to creep in. But when you fill that space instead with love—genuine love—for helping people by giving them the benefit of your expertise through your presentation, you are focused on benefits to others instead of yourself. What's

more important is how you will serve your audience. Ask yourself: How will my words benefit people's lives? When writing your speech, communicate those benefits and give your audience a reason to care about the words you say. When you can communicate how your speech can change someone's life, they are more likely to be engaged with the words you have to say.

4. **Practice makes perfect progress.** When you are comfortable with your material and your topic, it's time to take it for a test drive. Practice your speech in front of a mirror, in front of your camera, in front of your peers in a workshop or mastermind group (such as those offered by Powerful Women Today). Plan what you will say or do. This will help reduce the tension. Going through your speech a few times will help you feel more confident and train you to keep good pacing, vocal variety, gestures, and eye contact—yes even in a virtual setting! Speak slowly, breathe, and smile!

We all experience fear from time to time. There can be no courage without fear. If the thought of speaking publicly makes you nervous, you are halfway there! You can feel both nervous AND ready to speak publicly! When you finally step on stage, take a deep breath and get ready to captivate the audience with all the preparation you have done.

Speaking is the best way to share your expertise, grow aware-ness about your brand, and gain new clients. And yet, speak-ing on stage, whether virtual or live, is something many people fear—especially if you have never done it before. Sometimes we feel more comfortable listening to others tell stories, and it can be hard to flip the switch and feel confident when other people get to listen to you.

Building your speaking skills is just like learning to draw, train-ing for a race, or learning a new hobby. You start small and build upon past efforts to reach new milestones. In addition to refining your speech, you also want to seek out opportunities to give it to new audiences!

Public speaking gets easier with practice and with proven strat-egies to overcome the obstacles. It takes courage to share your expertise to help others. With practice and preparation, you can confidently embrace speaking in public, whether it be in a virtual summit, at a professional association, or on a conference main stage. You've got this.

30 DAY CHALLENGE: UNMUTE YOURSELF

The best way to overcome stage fright is to get on more stages with a speech you are confident presenting. The more experience that you have presenting your speech to an audience, the more familiar and comfortable being on a virtual or live stage will be.

As any experienced speaker will tell you, it's possible to be nervous AND a good speaker at the same time. The important thing is to take action and get your message out there!

Days 1–10: Speech writing

1. **MINDSET:** *I DO WHATEVER IT TAKES TO PREPARE MY PRE-SENTATIONS TO PERFECTION.* I am a natural at public speaking. I love to engage with the audience. I develop skills for effective communication. I take classes in presentation skills. I read books on public speaking. I learn about the different styles of speaking. I work on my elocution. I practice in front of a mirror.

2. **PLAN:** There are a number of blueprints you can follow when crafting your speech. One simple framework is: Introduce yourself with a personal story that relates to why you are in your field, cover 3 teaching points that solve a problem for your ideal audience. Make a call to action. And close with a personal story that illustrates the "after" benefits of following the 3 teaching points you covered.

3. **DO:** Set aside 15-30 minutes each day to work on crafting your speech. Write a 5–10 minute speech following your preferred blueprint

4. **CHECK:** Read through what you have written. Are your stories relevant to your teaching points? Do your teaching points align with your area of expertise, and do they solve a problem for your listeners? Do you have a call to action to encourage engagement after your speech is over? (Examples: subscribe to my podcast, email me for my free eBook, etc.)

5. **ADJUST:** Continue to edit your speech until you feel ready to get feedback from trusted peers and mentors in the next step.

Days 11-20: Speech practicing

1. **MINDSET:** *I TAKE ALL THE TIME I NEED TO STUDY AND PRACTICE MY PRESENTATIONS.* I seek good feedback from professional presenter mentors. I ask for help from motivational speaking coaches and presenters. I apply their ideas immediately and am open to honest and constructive feedback. I develop my own presentation style and adjust my presentations to my audience. The more I do presentations, the better I get.

2. **DO:** Practice your speech in front of a full-length mirror. Pay attention to your natural hand gestures and other body movements. Record yourself. Practice giving your speech to trusted friends and family, or in your networking group or your next speaker's workshop.

3. **CHECK:** Watch the video of yourself performing. Listen to the audio of your speech. Get feedback from your group. Take note of any filler words (um, uh, so, you know...) so you can work to remove them from your presentation. Note your vocal tone and tempo, and your body movements.

4. **ADJUST:** Practice your speech to work on areas for improvement. Revise the speech to add more detail for your audience where needed, and to remove the parts that don't seem to align with your teaching points. Add in, or tone down, gestures as appropriate. Consider your body language while you deliver your speech. Does it match the tone of your story?

5. **ADJUST:** Perform your speech again, making the changes you noted in your self-review and from the feedback of your trusted peers.

Days 21-30: Speech Delivery

1. **MINDSET:** *I GAIN CONFIDENCE THE MORE I PUT MYSELF OUT THERE.* We show up to your speech to learn from you. You have the honor of sharing your knowledge to make our lives better, and you come to the stage to share with us from a place of service and of love.

2. **PLAN:** Time to take the show on the road. Identify places where you can deliver your speech to groups. Start small! Even experienced speakers will address groups of 10 or so.

   » **Where to find your next audience?** Reach out to event organizers on MeetUp and offer to share your knowledge. Many churches let authors and members speak at special events. Associations and network groups have monthly meetings that welcome speakers. Specialty stores that align with your brand (spirituality, yoga and wellness studios, bookstores, home improvement) have special events where experts in the same field share their knowledge. Contact the management! Find professional associations on LinkedIn and reach out to their meeting planners. Get involved in one of Powerful Women Today's Women Empowerment Summits.

3. **DO:** Reach out to the event organizers for your identified group(s) and ask if you can set a time to share your knowledge.

4. **CHECK:** Is the event you are presenting for being promoted? How many are expected to attend? Does your speech include teaching points and a call to action specific to this audience?

5. **ADJUST:** You have rehearsed and refined your speech now. So, instead of bringing the full script, jot down some talking points to help you in your delivery. Is your venue set up to accommodate your visuals? If not, that's ok – make a handout or revise your speech so you don't need to rely on your slide deck.

Congratulations! You've done it! From blank page to improving the lives of your audience in 30 days.

About the Author

MARIANNE BJELKE (bee-ell-kuh), The Business Communication Strategist, is the host and mentor to the very first Powerful Women Today chapter in the United States, located in the beautiful high-desert region of Albuquerque, New Mexico.

The founder of Strategic Business Solutions Consulting, Marianne understands how the nuances of communication impact running a profitable business. Her clients turn to her for increased awareness of perspective bias, communication styles, generational influences, and more – awareness which helps them blast through the, often unseen, barriers to true communication and impact.

A stand-up comedian in NYC at age 21, she settled down and opened her first successful business, Herb'N Trends – a retail herb, tea, and gift shop, at just 25 years old. Moving cross-country two years later allowed Marianne to pursue a new passion; programming and software development. She quickly grew this into an executive management career, enjoying over 15 years in healthcare information management before striking out on her own. Marianne has successfully managed award-winning

7-figure revenue-generating projects from concept and design, through the development stages and into launch.

Working with cross-functional teams ignited her passion for helping ALL project stakeholders (developers, designers, marketing teams, end users, and executive stakeholders) speak the same mission-driven language to effectively define goals and complete projects on time, on spec, and on budget.

CONTACT INFORMATION:

Find Marianne Bjelke at her website: **www.bewhatnow.com**

Join Marianne's Patreon group to gain access to tools, worksheets, and tailored coaching that will help you position your business for massive growth: **www.Patreon.com/MarianneBjelke**

Or go deeper and apply for a complimentary one-on-one strategy call: **www.BusinessCommunicationStrategy.com**

Marlenne Doss

Dedication

To my boys, Malakai and Noah, who inspire me and give me purpose to do what I do. To my husband, Paul, whose encouragement has carried me and our family every day. My love for all of you runs endless and deep. And to my sister, Marcelle, who has walked this journey side by side with me every day and continues to be my greatest cheerleader. I am blessed beyond measure and overflowing with gratitude for all of you.

Breaking Through Barriers To Success

by Marlenne Doss

Allow me to introduce myself. I am a mother, a daughter, a sister, a wife and a lawyer by profession. I wear many hats on any given day and each of my different roles have impacted my journey to where I am now. I have recently partnered with another phenomenal woman, and we started what we believe will be a gamechanger in the legal profession called Aion Law Partners LLP.

But like many of you, I am sure, the road was and likely continues to be bumpy at times. Gratefully, I have acquired a great deal of peace, skill, wisdom and strength that allow me to face challenges differently than I had in the past. Not that I always get it perfect, but it is about the growth, is it not? I continue to learn something new every day.

Looking back now, a few moments stand out that could have easily changed the course of my life. There were some very challenging and fear invoking situations that, had I allowed them to, would have stopped me in my tracks.

Growing up, my household included my parents, older sister, younger brother, and my uncle from my dad's side. When I was in high school, about 15 years old, my uncle had a severe stroke that really shook our lives. Shortly after, just as I was entering university for my undergraduate degree, my dad was diagnosed with Amyotrophic Lateral Sclerosis (ALS, otherwise known as Lou Gehrig's Disease). Our family battled it for the next decade, and it felt like the bottom was falling out constantly.

In my early twenties I faced my first real barrier: myself. Well, to be specific, my self-image. It was quite negative. It took me a long time to realize that the image I held of myself was not true or accurate. I had been looking outside, comparing myself inaccurately to others and internalizing criticism and self-doubt. All this contributed to the negative "movie reel," as I call it, that I was playing in my mind every day, all day.

It was not until I learned and understood that my confidence, my self-image, should be based in the truth that I am created by a perfect, loving God, in His image and that He abided in me that I was able to begin to change my perception of myself. I also came to understand that if I am made in His image, then disliking myself was rejecting His creation and the truth about Him. It was a process to replace that negative reel I had allowed to play for years. But it was necessary in order to begin to fulfill my purpose and pursue what I wanted. It was necessary in order to be able to really serve others.

Fast-forward a few years and I had to decide what career I wanted. I decided that I was going to stick with my original plan of going into law. So, while juggling university, helping to take care of my dad, and working part-time, I took the entrance exam, then faced the overwhelming process of applying to law schools. I had to make those financial and stressful investments in scarcity and literally *"let go and let God."*

Then the unexpected happened. I actually got accepted to law school. And with great joy came great terror. Not only of the prospect of moving away and actually going to law school, but the guilt and fear of thinking about how could I possibly leave my family to take care of my dad without me? It would be a great sacrifice from everyone, and I could not stomach it. To my family, it was not even a question—I was going. But my inner turmoil was crippling. I had to decide quickly whether I was going to accept the offer.

I had a conversation with one of my friends' dad. He told me that I was not supposed to stop moving forward and put my life on hold because of what was going on with my dad. So, I accepted, facing and conquering my next barrier to success.

I began my journey through law school and loved it. However, things at home continued to be challenging and I was not always the best student. I got some grades I was not proud of and faced my next fork in the road. I could not get my license to practice law unless after law school I found an articling placement. I had been told that even a couple of lower marks would restrict me from this. So, in my second year of law school, I considered dropping out and walking away. Why continue to be away from home for another year if I was not even going to get a license at the end?

By grace, I had wisdom enough to speak with our Student Advisor before throwing in the towel. Again, by grace, she advised me to stay the course and reassured me I would find an articling position. So, I chose to trust the process and continued to step out in faith, believing that a way would be made, and it was. I graduated from law school, found and completed my articling position and received my license to practice as a lawyer.

Upon becoming a lawyer, I had to find a job but I did not want to settle on a job that did not meet my primary goal of using my career in order to serve others. I deliberately ignored job postings that could clear my school debts and only applied to positions that I really wanted, which were not many. I did not get any of them. Then people in my community started asking me to help them with their legal matters. So, I ended up starting my own practice, which I had no plans of doing. Nor did I have the resources, including the know-how, to run a business. That was the last leap that put me on the course to where I am now.

I am so grateful for all my experiences and all the lessons I learned along the way. One of the lessons is that I really do not need to know "how" things are going to work, I just need to decide what I want, what I am passionate about, and the rest works itself out. I am so grateful that I am still being stretched daily. I am so grateful that I do not resist as much as I used to. I am so grateful for all the wonderful people that I cross paths with. I am grateful if I can use what I have learned to help someone else.

I am sharing my story here to encourage you to break through your own barriers, to know that you can face whatever fears you may have and achieve whatever it is that you really want. I truly believe that if I can do it, anyone can! Whatever it is, decide that you are going to do it, step into it in faith and watch as the doors swing wide open. It will take perseverance to stick it out, but know that you are capable and are meant to succeed. The world needs each of us to stop playing small.

ACTIVITIES:

Week 1 — What's playing on your "movie reel"?

Take some time to sit with yourself and really listen to the subconscious messages you play to yourself. Is there room for improvement? If so, make a list of your negative self-talk. Then, next to each item, write a replacement sentence that is positive and affirming. Continue to pay close attention to these passive thoughts and make a conscious effort to stop your mind from racing with them. When you hear one, say to yourself "hold on there!" and replace it with a positive affirmation. You may not believe them at first, but continue to remind yourself that they are true and continue to write them down repeatedly daily, even many times daily, until your movie reel changes. This will certainly take more than a week, it may take more than 30 days and you may need help from someone else. But start it and do not stop until you win this battle with yourself. You cannot achieve the greatness you deserve and are meant for without confidence. You will not gain this confidence unless you are drawing on it from what I believe is the truth, that we are spiritual beings and created by a perfect creator.

Week 2 – What do you really want?

Is there a goal or desire that you have and perhaps have not had the courage to pursue? If so, write it down and read it every day at least twice a day. Believe that it is something you will receive. Picture yourself having it or being in the role. Use your imagination to see yourself with it now.

Then write out in detail what you need to achieve this goal. It does not matter if you have the resources now to obtain it or even that you know where they will come from. What is necessary is having a clear vision of this desire and being emotionally connected with it.

If you are having difficulty naming something, then take some time every day to sit with yourself and explore what it is you really want. What would you be happiest doing? What service do you want to provide? As you get closer to finding it, your emotional connection to it should be palpable. Your motivation to get it and desire to do whatever it takes to have it will also grow. I believe that is when the resources will begin to present themselves to you.

Week 3 – What is your barrier?

I am fairly certain that many of you that have read my story, which just scrapes the surface of my experiences, can relate to facing a huge fear before doing something new that feels bigger than anything you have done before. Or perhaps you are experiencing this fear now that you have found what it is you want.

If you have had to face such a fear before, write down your story, paying close attention to the barrier you faced and how you overcame it. Try to identify the tools and strategies you developed to get through it. Note how they can help you the next time you are faced with your next barrier, because there will certainly be a next time if you continue to evolve.

Now, take a look at what you wrote down during week 2 that you really want. What fears are standing in your way of receiving it? Determine that you will push through those barriers and take at least one step this week in the direction of what you want, regardless of how small it is. Once that task is done, move onto the next one, and so on. Do this keeping a clear picture of what you are pursuing and continuing to attach your emotions with this goal.

Week 4 — Repetition

During this last week, take stock of where you started and where you find yourself now. You are likely feeling that you are still at the beginning of your journey, which is expected. If your goal or your plan to achieve it needs tweaking, do that now and rewrite your goal in detail.

My hope for you is that you are approaching your current circumstances from a place of faith and hope, with a determination that you will reach your goals and an understanding that you are capable and deserving.

Be sure to seek the resources and counsel you need on your way and find an accountability partner that can help you stick to your plans. Just be wise with who you share your greatest dreams with.

But most importantly, enjoy the journey and be grateful for it.

If you would like to learn more about me or Aion Law Partners LLP, visit us at www.aionlaw.ca and like and follow us on Instagram and Facebook. If I can offer you any services that will help you achieve your goals, please get in touch.

About the Author

Growing up **MARLENNE** always thought she would pursue a career in law because she was highly motivated by a desire to help people. This same desire is what compelled her to write this chapter.

Marlenne received her LL.B. from Queen's University in 2004 and was called to the bar in 2005. She is a member of the Law Society of Ontario and brings a breadth of experience to her practice. She has appeared before the Ontario Superior Court, the Federal Court of Appeal, and various tribunals

including the Immigration and Refugee Board. She founded her own practice in 2008, specializing in the areas of real estate, wills and estates, corporate and immigration law. In 2021, she established Aion Law Partners LLP as a founding partner. Aion Law prides itself on providing the service and experience of a large firm without losing the personal touch and compassion of a small firm.

Marlenne is passionate about empowering community members to understand pertinent legal topics related to everyday life. She volunteers her time by providing seminars on various legal matters to her community and to a wide range of businesses. Marlenne considers her faith and family to be most important to her. She enjoys traveling, cooking, the theatre, and cultural activities. Marlenne loves to encourage other women and firmly believes each woman can break any barriers in her way to reach her full potential.

CONTACT INFORMATION

Marlenne Doss
Aion Law Partners LLP
info@aionlaw.ca
http://linkedin.com/in/marlenne-doss-90564120
https://www.aionlaw.ca

Marsha Gleit

Dedication

I dedicate this chapter to all the courageous women who have stepped outside their comfort zone to accomplish amazing things. I especially acknowledge my mom, Phyllis and my daughter, Danielle, from whom I have learned so much.

Microsoft was my Goliath ... What's Yours?

by Marsha Gleit

As the door closed behind me, I could hear my great-niece come running down the hallway to meet me.

"Aunt Marsha, Aunt Marsha," she called out. *"Do you remember the story of David and Goliath? I just heard the story on the Google machine you gave me."*

I laughed. She still called the Google Home we gave her three years earlier, the Google machine. But as we talked about the bible story, all I could think about was how I could relate to David. I had recently given a talk at Microsoft and, as I prepared for that speech, I couldn't understand why this talk made me more nervous than usual. It was at that moment that it all came clear. I was David and I would have to, and did, conquer Goliath.

In the story, David knew size didn't matter. It was his heart, courage, and commitment that mattered. You can apply that same principle and same level of thinking to life and the challenges we all face. Think bigger than the challenge, be bigger than the obstacle, and act as if you can't fail. I did face the challenge and gave the talk of my young speaking career. And I attribute my success to my self-confidence and happiness. So, what if your happiness and self-confidence determine your success?

HAPPINESS:

By definition, happiness is a state of well-being and contentment or joy. One way of calculating your happiness is by using the happiness quotient formula.

- ❖ On a scale of one to ten, determine what is your willingness to learn (and you cannot grade yourself a five)?
- ❖ Next, on a scale of one to ten, what is your willingness to change or give something up?
- ❖ Lastly, multiply the two numbers together and this is your quotient.

The more you are willing to change and learn, the greater your score and the greater your happiness. The happiness quotient can be applied to any area of your life.

- ❖ Your overall happiness
- ❖ Your relationship with your spouse or children
- ❖ Your job or career
- ❖ Your relationship with money

You get the picture.

SELF-CONFIDENCE:

Self-confidence, by definition, is a feeling of trust in one's abilities, qualities, and judgment. Self-confidence can be interchanged with self-esteem and self-love. Putting yourself first attributes to your self-confidence. Taking care of you, physically, emotionally, and spiritually. By implementing self-care strategies like keeping a gratitude journal, believing in God or energy from the universe, eating a healthy diet, regular exercise, and hydration can increase your dopamine and cortisol levels, which can boost your self-confidence.

SUCCESS:

Success, by definition, is the accomplishment of an aim or purpose. Success means something different to each of us.

How do you define success?

- ❖ Is it a monetary value? The amount of money in the bank, the amount of money you make, or earning 6 or 7 figures in your business?
- ❖ Is success determined by your career or your title?
- ❖ Is it determined by your education or degrees?

- ❖ Or is it determined by your family, relationships, or social status?

For some, it is a combination of some or all of the above.

David's success comes from toppling Goliath. Taking a rock in his slingshot and hitting the giant. And then he fell. When Goliath fell, so did the Philistines. He was successful. He was happy and his self-confidence was increased. I was self-confident, I was happy, and it led to my successful talk at Microsoft.

How does this apply to your life or your business? Happiness, self-confidence, and success are not points on a triangle. Instead, they are points along a circle. A continuous circle. The rounder the circle, like the wheels on a bike, the smoother the ride.

How can you apply these concepts to your life and find the courage to act and follow through?

The Webster's dictionary defines courage as *"the ability to do something that frightens one."* It is my belief, which has been proven through my years of experience, that courage is synonymous with self-confidence and self-love and finding the balance within the circle that was described above. I came to this realization as more and more of my clients started their journey towards self-care and becoming the best they could be. In my book, Putting Yourself First, Supports Those Around You, 30 Days to a Healthier, Wealthier, Supportive You, I describe how you can accomplish anything you put your mind to. When we fear something, we lack the courage to act. But when we want something bad enough, it can be accomplished.

Here is a four (4) week roadmap that can be applied to any situation you may find yourself in that takes the courage that you may believe you're lacking.

Week One:

1. Clearly define the "WHAT" – What is it you want to do? Is it losing weight, landing that next big client, or beginning a new career or job? What is it? Set that goal for yourself and post it everywhere.

2. What will it feel like when you accomplish that goal? Can you see it? Can you feel it? Can you taste it? Can you touch it? Can you smell it? All your senses come alive when you focus on that goal.

3. List what you will need to do to overcome the obstacles. What stands in your way? Maybe it's your love for chocolate, the prospective client's current vendor, or you don't have

the perfect skillset? These obstacles are not your internal fears, they are concrete and anyone wanting to accomplish the same goal would have the same obstacle. Think of it as being on the same playing field.

Write the answers to the three items above in a journal as you may want to reference them later.

Week Two:

Here you will begin to implement your self-care strategies. Putting yourself first. I have written before about five minutes a day to self-care. It can begin with a nighttime routine or a morning routine. I like to focus on a nighttime routine. A good night's sleep Is one of the most important things you can do for yourself. This routine can be as easy as turning off your cell phone and television, creating a soothing atmosphere by play-ing some quiet music, diffusing your favorite oils, or even some simple meditation. The goal is to separate the day from the night.

Write in your journal your self-care plan and each day affirm that you completed the tasks on your plan.

Week Three:

Continue your self-care routine and add an additional 5 minutes a day by taking some time in nature, taking a five-minute brisk walk, practicing affirmations in the mirror, or a self-massage while taking a shower.

Now that you know exactly what you want to do and you are feeling much better about yourself by taking at least five minutes a day for you and just you, you are ready to start busting the obstacle list that you created in week one.

1. Review the obstacle list and set a plan for overcoming that obstacle.

2. Begin with the item that you believe to be the hardest.

3. Look at the obstacle from an outsider's perspective, without your own self-doubt getting in the way. This is just a plan. You are not implementing the plan at this point. The purpose is to think outside your comfort zone. Eliminating the "I can't do that" syndrome. This plan can be as simple or as detailed as you deem necessary.

Week Four:

Continue your self-care routine and continue to add an additional five minutes a day by taking some time in nature, taking a five-minute brisk walk, practicing affirmations in the mirror, or a self-massage while taking a shower.

You are almost at the finish line.

1. Review the lists from week one, giving attention to item number 2. Can you visualize how you will feel when you accomplish your goal. Can you use each of your five senses? Close your eyes as this may help.

2. Review each of the plans you created on the obstacle's list from week three.

3. Implement the plan by beginning with the one you believe is the most difficult for you. This should be done without the "I can't do it" syndrome. Any time that your mind goes down the rabbit hole of I can't do it, remind yourself you can. Repeat out loud I CAN DO IT and any other affirmation that works for you. Remind yourself that you have the skills, you have the tools, you have the courage.

You do have the courage. You have built your self-confidence through implementation of your self-care plan. You have found balance, your circle of happiness, self-confidence and success. Eliminating your fear – finding your courage.

About the Author

MARSHA GLEIT was born in Queens, NY and raised in Wayne, NJ. She now resides in Irvine, CA with her wonderful husband Bruce of 34 years. They have two adult children, Danielle 30, and Max 25. Marsha holds a B.A. in Business / Economics from University of California Santa Barbara, and an MBA in Finance from Pace University in NY. She is also a Certified Life Coach and CA Real Estate Broker. Marsha Gleit spent a 30-year career span in corporate finance and accounting. Marsha volunteers as a SCORE Mentor and recently has published a book called, 'You Can't Be Good For Them Until You're Good To You.' Marsha is the Founder and CEO of Levity Leadership for the past five years.

Marsha's experience as a corporate leader, mentor, and sitting on board of directors' on both the profit and non-profit side, made her aware of the need for impact on a much bigger scale. When Marsha was hospitalized for a blood infection that led to the amputation of 3 toes, she realized what was missing in her life and the lives of those she worked with. Her realization of self-care applied to all. It was at that moment that she began practicing and teaching self-care strategies to leaders and entrepreneurs so that they too, could create a happier, self-confident, and productive life.

Marsha Gleit now travels the world both virtually and to live events helping men and women personally and professionally understand the importance of self-care and development of their human skills, and the ramifications of the contrary. She shares her unique four step strategy and shows them how to Get Everything They Want so that they can catch their bright shining star in their ongoing success.

CONTACT INFORMATION

Marsha Gleit
Levity Leadership
Founder & CEO
marsha@burgeoncoaching.com
https://www.linkedin.com/in/marsha-gleit-mhg

"

"I believe in being strong when everything seems to be going wrong, I believe that happy girls are the prettiest girls. I believe that tomorrow is another day, and I believe in miracles."

—Audrey Hepburn

Melanie Herschorn

Dedication

For my daughter Deanna and my son Nicholas who inspire me

every day.

30 Days to Amplifying Your Voice

by Melanie Herschorn

Have you ever planned a big event, chosen a fabulous venue, a top-notch caterer, gorgeous flowers, and the perfect outfit, and then not sent out any invitations for guests to attend?

I hope not! That would be a terrible waste of your time and money. I feel so bad for all those uneaten canapés.

But something similar is happening every day to business owners who work tirelessly to write a book and then don't spend time marketing it.

Authors often get so wrapped up in the writing, editing, and publishing process that by the time the book is ready for purchase, they're burned out. They don't know how to get it into the hands of their ideal readers so they give up and move on, leaving a stack of books with their name on it to collect dust.

I firmly believe that if you have a mission that fuels you and you've birthed a book meant to become your calling card—a way to help you become a thought leader in your industry, fill your courses and programs, and help you speak on stages— then it's your right to tell the world about it. In fact, I think you owe it to yourself and the readers whose lives you can change to keep going. Your work isn't done when you give birth to a baby. You have to raise it too. That's where book marketing comes in.

There should be no shame in shouting from the rooftops how amazing you are for becoming an author and sharing your gifts with the people you want to help, especially since the statistics floated in writers circles are that 97 percent of writers never finish their books. So if you've beaten the odds and published a book, no matter if you went the self, hybrid, or traditional publishing route, you should already see that you've got something special.

Any time you write from the heart and share intimate moments of your life, you may step into an uncomfortable space. Having been vulnerable on the pages may cause you to shy away from ever sharing your work because, what will people think?

But that vulnerability makes you and your story real and relatable. Your authenticity and courage to share part of your life will separate you from the competition. Sure, it can be scary to put yourself out there, first on the pages of your book and then on Instagram, but you owe it to yourself and your book to try. Need a nudge? Revisit your mission. Your mission is what will get you out of bed in the morning ready to share your message each and every day.

DISCOVERING MY MISSION

My first job out of grad school was as an afternoon news anchor and general assignment reporter at a radio station in Pennsylvania. I was the only woman in a newsroom of men and felt like a fish out of water coming from Los Angeles to a city of 50 thousand people.

At station-sponsored events which I was obligated to attend, I'd often get backhanded compliments like, *"you're sounding a bit better"* or *"you don't sound as new anymore,"* and sometimes outright insults about me and my reporting. At least no one ever told me I had a face for radio! Whenever I made a mistake live on the air, my news director would come running toward me from the newsroom, ready to reprimand me. Since the entire radio booth was glass, I could see when I was about to get it.

With such constant scrutiny, (one senator's campaign manager spent 20 minutes screaming at me over a misunderstanding), I developed a pretty thick skin. I soon stopped worrying about what other people thought of me because I realized that no matter what I did, I couldn't please everyone. Armed with that protective shell, I decided to pursue a new purpose: to tell the stories of the underserved. While I still covered the stories assigned to me, whenever my news director gave me a little freedom, I would highlight issues about women and children, doing my best to give them a voice on our male-dominated airwaves.

I did an in-depth report about a camp for young children who'd had a parent pass away, a series on the wives of senatorial candidates, and a three-part story on teens in the PA foster care system. I'm proud to say that these stories garnered journalism awards, but the most rewarding part was the gratitude from those featured in the stories.

When I was 5 months pregnant with my first child, I was abruptly laid off from the station. At that point in my life, my entire identity had been wrapped up in my being a journalist, and without that position I felt like I was nothing. What's more, reporters from other news outlets began calling me to ask why I'd been laid off. I'd become the story.

As luck would have it, I wasn't unemployed for long. The local newspaper scooped me up and brought me on to cover an inner-city school district that was having serious budgetary woes, so I still got to report and give a voice to the voiceless.

Soon entrepreneurship began calling to me. When we moved to Arizona, I developed a line of breastfeeding shirts and dresses for nursing moms. Not really a normal trajectory, I know. Still, I singlehandedly grew the brand and within a few years my products were being sold in boutiques across North America, on Amazon and on Nordstrom's website.

My favorite part of my business was marketing my "stuff" and I really wanted to get better at it. So, I hired a woman that I'd worked with in another capacity to help me. She claimed to be an internet marketing expert who could help me make my brand a household name. That was the beginning of the end of the company. She became verbally and emotionally abusive toward me, constantly telling me that my ideas were boring and that there was no way I could ever do the marketing myself. But I felt stuck. She had me believing I needed her and I feared repercussions if I tried to sever our working relationship. Over the course of a year, I paid her around $25,000. I walked away with 5000 Instagram followers who were never going to buy from my brand, and very low self-esteem. I shut down the business shortly thereafter.

AMPLIFYING YOUR VOICE

After some introspection and talking with friends and my life coach at the time, I knew that I had to turn that awful experience into something positive. I found my voice and my mission again. When I looked back at my career up to that point, I saw that I'd truly developed a skillset to support women business owners with their marketing. I also tallied that I'd done about 10,000 hours of it, which author Malcolm Gladwell has made famous for being the number of hours it takes to become proficient at a skill. I originally opened my current company, VIP Digital Content, to ensure that other business owners would stop being misled by marketers making all sorts of promises. And over time, the mission has evolved to include helping to amplify authors' voices to make the world a better place.

It took a lot of courage for me to start another company.

It took a lot of courage for me to stand in my power and say that I'm good at marketing.

It also takes courage for you to promote your book and your accomplishments as an author across social media, emails, podcasts, more. But if you've written a book, you're absolutely entitled to be recognized as an authority in your field and grow your online influence.

And that is what I get to help authors do every single day. One of my favorite things about being a journalist was that no two days were ever the same. That's one of the things that I adore about working with authors, no two books are alike and the sky's the limit for what you can achieve when you develop a fan base of your ideal audience.

Putting yourself out there to market your book and your brand doesn't have to feel like you're standing naked in a room full of strangers. I'm here to help.

Here are steps that you can take today to begin building your VIP author platform online. Then you'll be well on your way to showing people that not only are you an expert, you wrote the book on it!

Step 1: Develop Your Marketing Mindset

Please give yourself some grace. It's not your fault that you may not know the steps to creating excitement around your book. I continually work on my skills by learning new marketing techniques and staying up-to-date with social media and email marketing developments. We are most productive when we stay in our zone of genius. But when it's time to market your book, you do have the power to do it successfully. You may just need some guidance.

To start, remind yourself that YOU are qualified:

* ❖ Your experiences are interesting and worthy of being shared
* ❖ You have a unique view and message that needs to get out in the world
* ❖ You have the power to change someone's life for the better with your book

Whenever you find yourself in a place of doubt, revisit your mission and tell your audience why you were inspired to write a book, what you hope they'll get from it, and what your mission and vision are. When you enroll your audience in your mission, your passion and vision will undoubtedly inspire them to become your raving fans.

Step 2: Tighten Your Messaging

The next requirement is to refine your messaging. To do this, you'll want to know who your ideal audience is so you can target your message to their needs. Speaking in generalities is a no-no because when you try talking to everybody, you end up talking to nobody.

Figure out who they are and then answer these questions: What do they want to hear from you? What advice can you impart to them? What words can you use that will truly resonate with them?

Step 3: Plan Your Content

Planning the what, when, and how you're going to amplify your message does take some time. But there are great resources that can help you make it a simpler and more streamlined process.

It's best to start with a content calendar (and you can grab a free, printable content calendar at the end of this chapter!). Use it to determine what content you're going to create to amplify your message, if possible, one quarter at a time. You can tie social media posts and emails to holidays, events, and national days. Once you have the photos and captions you'll be posting, you can load them into a platform like Planoly, Buffer, Hootsuite, Later, or Facebook's Creator Studio and set them to post automatically for you.

Step 4: Be Consistent

Positioning yourself as an expert online also requires consistency. You're the go-to expert in your space but no one will know if you don't continually tell them. Posting something once on social media and walking away doesn't immediately result in book sales.

You have to show up for your audience each and every week – both on social media and on email. When you are reliable, your audience will truly get to know, like, and trust you. That is why they will ultimately buy from you.

Unfortunately, social media algorithms are not your friend. As few as 2 percent of your followers may be seeing your posts. That's why adding email marketing into your overall marketing strategy is a good idea. When you send emails, you stay top of mind and you'll know if people have opened them.

Following these four steps will give you the foundation you desire to become the go-to expert in your industry. But sticking to them requires an element of accountability that not everyone innately has. So that's why finding an accountability partner or coach to support you will make all the difference.

When I work with authors, my goal is to become their cheerleader, guide, and marketing support system. I strive to help them learn, grow, and develop their authority online. Marketing is a long game. It takes time to create your VIP author platform and begin to see the fruits of your labor. But sticking with it is vital to positioning yourself as the influencer in your space you deserve to be.

Ready to begin planning your content? Get a free, printable Content Calendar here: https://vipdigital.live/courage

About the Author

MELANIE HERSCHORN wants to make your book and brand sparkle online. As a content marketing strategist for coaches, consultants, and speakers worldwide, she's on a mission to support and empower her clients to create clear messaging and content that shines a light on their individuality, skillset, and books. With her unique combination of entrepreneurship, award-winning journalism and PR experience, Melanie guides her clients to attract and nurture leads and position themselves as industry experts. She also loves to give book marketing tips on her live show Authority Marketing Live!

CONTACT INFORMATION

Melanie Herschorn
Book Marketing Strategist & Coach
https://www.linkedin.com/in/melanie-herschorn-a8122126/
https://www.facebook.com/groups/vipdigitalmarketingtips/
vipdigitalcontent.com
melanie@vipdigitalcontent.com

"
"If you don't love me at my worst, then you don't deserve me at my best."
—Marilyn Monroe

Mindy Gillis

Dedication

My chapter, Marylin, My Mom, and Me, in 30 Days to Courage is dedicated to my Mom and Marylin Monroe, and others like them, who are talented and smart women who have yet to overcome their fears.

Marilyn, My Mom, and Me

MY JOURNEY TO A COURAGEOUS LIFE

by Mindy Gillis

Courage!?! What is it? What does it mean? Courage is the ability to move forward in the face of fear and uncertainty. Well, that is my definition. We all have hopes, dreams, and fears. It is the fear that keeps us from doing things we shouldn't be doing but fear also can paralyze us, keeping us from moving towards our goals and aspirations. How often have you let fear or uncertainty hold you back? Many of us do not realize how much fear has gotten in our way. Our natural tendency is to brush it off as excuses and play the victim. This helps our brain make sense of why we did what we did or didn't do, what we wanted or knew we needed to do. As humans, we have a hard time realizing that it is our own thoughts, reactions, and fear that is what is really getting in our way.

I remember a time when I was young and staying at my grand-mother's house during the summer. My mom dropped me and my brother there and we had no idea if she was going to come back for us. My grandmother, on my father's side, was not a nice person. She loved my brother but didn't like me. She said it was because I reminded her of my mother. She was a six-foot 300lb German woman with a distain for my mother. One day, I got in trouble for walking in the house with grass sticking to my feet. I cleaned it up, but my grandmother felt that a good beating with a yardstick would do the trick. Let's just say that she broke the yard stick on my back and butt. I cried for hours. I didn't understand. Why!?! Why did this woman hate me so much? Why would my mother make me go back there time after time? Then I heard a still small voice talk to me and tell me everything was going to be alright. That I was destined to do great things and that one day, I wouldn't have to live in fear anymore. I knew, from that day on, that I didn't have to stay poor. That I could be different from my family and move towards my destiny. I had this renewed sense of purpose and vigor towards creating a better life for me.

I grew up very poor. I remember so many cockroaches and dumpy places to live. I didn't realize how little privilege I had when I was growing up until I got into diversity work at a healthcare organization. When they came to our team, we went through a diversity exercise where you would put an x on the items that were considered to be part of one's life as a privilege (example: I had more than 10 books in my home growing up). Out of 25 items, I only had five Xs. My colleagues had 18 or more. I was shocked as I didn't realize how little privilege I had. I knew I had less than my friends in school but not to that extent. Privilege is subjective and so is fear.

Fear is this small, four-letter word and yet it has so much power over most of us. It was meant to keep us safe and out of harm's way but now it shows up in every aspect of our life as worry, anxiety, and depression. I've seen this on social media and I don't know who created these acronyms but they are powerful. Fear: False Evidence Appearing Real. When I first saw this on social media it resonated with me. It helped me to reframe fear into something that is tangible and perspective changing. Fear is an internal emotion that we create based on the thoughts that we have. Read that again. We create our own fear. We do this unknowingly by the thoughts that we choose to have about a situation. How many times have you allowed fear to keep you from your best? What was the falsehood in your thoughts?

I started working when I was fourteen years old. It was then that I was able to meet other people and see that they were happy and successful. I then realized that there was another way. Then slowly, as I became more aware of how my negativity and anger was affecting those around me, I started looking for people who exemplified the life I knew I was destined to have. The fear of staying in the same circumstances outweighed the fear of reaching out and talking to people and asking what they did to get where they were. The more I put myself out there, the more that people wanted to help.

One of my worst days turned into a huge pivotal point for me. My friend was brave enough to tell me that how I thought I showed up and how people perceived me was completely different. I was devastated and took it really hard. Some people would've held a grudge or gave excuses but I knew this was what was getting in my way. I did cry. I did have a pity party and that is ok. What I chose to do was to figure out what I needed to do to ensure that the person who I wanted to show up as was the person that was perceived by others. My need to not ever go back to the circumstances that I came from kept me moving and growing. Fear can be a positive thing, but only if it helps you to move in a positive direction.

Over the past twenty-five years, I have worked on myself. I have dedicated my life to helping others learn and grow as I have. I am constantly working on being as self-reflective as I can. It is the cornerstone of how I have gotten to where I am today. I not only reflect on myself but I also ask for feedback. When we realize that feedback is a gift, we tend to ask for it more often. Becoming an executive coach is one of the best things I could've done for myself. The very nature of coaching is the type of leader that I want to be. I want to be a leader that inspires, listens, and helps others overcome their challenges in life.

In my coaching business, I work with many women who are talented and brilliant but they don't see that in themselves. Despite the work they have done, they still feel inadequate. I wonder if this is how Marylin Monroe felt? I've always been a fan of Marylin Monroe and wish I was there to help her see how amazing she was. It makes me wonder why so many women allow their fear to overtake them. I guess I was lucky growing up the way I did because it felt like everything was going up from where I came from. I grew a thick skin at a very young age. I didn't care what others thought about me, until I got into corporate America. I ended up in the emergency room two weeks into my new job in corporate America due to severe anxiety. There was my fear and anger showing up again but this time it was affecting my body and my heart. Was it the pressure to be perfect that got to Marylin? Was it that she cared so much about what people thought of her? Or was it that she had been told over and over that she wasn't good enough by the people who were around her from birth? I believe it is a combination of all three. We don't start our lives with self-defeating thoughts. They are taught to us by our parents, teachers, etc. We do not have to be a victim to our thoughts. We get to choose to challenge our thoughts. We get to choose a different perspective. What if Marylin had a coach who helped her to see that it was her own thoughts about herself that was driving her fear?

My mother is a talented artist. She started painting when she was married to her third husband. He made enough money so that my mom didn't have to work. I was about to become a teenager at this point in time. I remember my mom always reaching for something better. I didn't realize it at the time, but she was doing the best she could to raise us. She always worked three jobs to keep us going. I never realized the courage she needed to keep us fed, clothed, and with a roof over our heads. Her courage came from the fear of losing her kids. Courage is not about not having fear but it is how we choose to use the fear to either propel us forward or hold us back. As I got older, my mom dreamed of becoming a famous artist. She would paint on canvas but then she taught herself ways to improve a home with paint instead of having to do a total renovation. She made some money on the side with this business, but it was her cleaning business that kept us afloat. I could never understand why she wouldn't go out and sell her paintings. I then realized that it was the same fear that propelled her forward that was holding her back.

Over the years, I have had the privilege to procure some of her artwork to put up in my office at work. I had my first office ever and then two years later, COVID hit. I had two of her paintings that I used in my coaching with leaders. One was a frog and the other was a turtle. I would talk about how great leadership is knowing when to be the frog with lots of energy and when to be the turtle. I don't know if my mom ever knew how those paintings impacted my coaching clients. Now, I work remotely in the healthcare organization that I've served for more than fifteen years and in my executive coaching business. My mom painted a picture of Marylin Monroe several years back and I have loved that painting for a long time but I was told that I couldn't have it. It was their favorite. After five years of trying to get the Marilyn painting, I was able to increase what I was willing to pay for it to one thousand dollars. That did it. I finally got the painting that I had always wanted. I didn't realize the effect it would have on my mom. She was so surprised and en-thusiastic. She never dreamed of selling one of her paintings for a thousand dollars and that I would pay that much for one of her paintings. That one purchase has inspired my mom to paint again. We never know how one little act of kindness can change others' lives.

Marylin, my mom, and me is about a lifetime of choosing to become better. Choosing to listen to feedback and make the changes. Choosing to focus on the positive instead of the negative. Choosing to see fear as false evidence appearing real. Choosing to set goals and go after them. Choosing to reach out when we need help. I didn't realize that Marylin is the person or persona that I chose to coach. I choose to coach those who are stuck in fear or feel they are inadequate. I help many of my clients both women and men, overcome the inner critic and imposter syndrome that plagues many of us.

Here are a few quotes from my clients on how I have helped them overcome their fear and become courageous.

"Mindy encouraged me to place my "entire" self into endeavors, stretching myself for growth. This took courage and was well worth the effort."

"Mindy reminded me that growth only occurs with change, and that change requires bravery. I think of this concept each time a new opportunity arises."

"Coaching taught me that it's ok – desirable, no less! – to have and express clear boundaries and expectations at work. This realization has given me the courage to push back when those boundaries are breached or verbalize when expectations are not met. Also, it has been helpful to be able to brainstorm various approaches to problem-solving and to rehearse future crucial conversations, as these exercises have improved my confidence when interacting with colleagues in my leadership roles."

"There are many perils a leader faces on a daily basis of different magnitudes. Leadership coaching has given me the courage to address potential impactful situations immediately and in partnership with key stakeholders before the situation is uncontrolled. Through leadership coaching, I learned how to be courageous and tackle difficult situations upfront with transparency, integrity and clear direction."

EXERCISES:

Week 1: Let's get real with ourselves

Answer the following questions below as a foundation for the rest of the month's exercises.

What is your life's purpose?

_____

_____

What fulfills you?

_____

_____

What scares you?

_____

_____

What are your top strengths?

_____

_____

What is missing in your life? What is getting in your way?

_____

_____

What do you typically procrastinate on?

_____

_____

What would you do if you couldn't fail?

_____

_____

Week 2: Journaling

Based on the questions you answered in week one, I'd like for you to start journaling and writing down when a self-defeating thought comes to you.

EXAMPLE:

DATE: Monday 2.21.22

SELF-DEFEATING THOUGHT: They will never pick me for that role so why even apply.

CIRCUMSTANCES: A new director role came available. I didn't get the other director roles.

DATE: Monday 2.21.22

SELF-DEFEATING THOUGHT: I don't want to speak up in this meeting because I am afraid to. Every time I say something, no one responds.

CIRCUMSTANCES: Bi-weekly team meeting where I've chosen not to speak up in due to lack of responses from the team.

Week 3: Reframe

How might you change your self-defeating thought to a positive thought?

Taking the list from week one and then taking time every day to create new thoughts that will empower you to choose action instead of fear.

DATE: Monday 2.21.22

SELF-DEFEATING THOUGHT: They will never pick me for that role so why even apply.

CIRCUMSTANCES: A new director role came available. I didn't get the other director roles.

REFRAME: Just because they haven't picked me yet, doesn't mean that I am not able. I need to make sure that I am interviewing at the top of my game and practice the interview this time.

DATE: Monday 2.21.22

SELF-DEFEATING THOUGHT: I don't want to speak up in this meeting because I am afraid to. Every time I say something, no one responds.

CIRCUMSTANCES: Bi-weekly team meeting where I've chosen not to speak up in due to lack of responses from the team.

REFRAME: Maybe it is how I bring things up in the meeting. Maybe I should speak to someone that I trust on my team to receive feedback?

Week 4:

Looking back on the work you've done for the first two weeks, now ask yourself these questions to help you think about what might take you from fear to freedom?

EXAMPLE:

How might you take the insights that you've uncovered above and create an action plan?

ACTION PLAN:

I have been procrastinating_____. I choose to do_____differently in order to overcome my fear and stop procrastinating. I plan to do this by _____. I will know and others will know that I've accomplished this because we will see _____. I will hold myself accountable by doing _____.

Overcoming fear and becoming more courageous is tough work. If you'd like help on your journey to becoming more courageous, please don't hesitate to reach out and set up a free 30-minute coaching call.

Artist: Sue Riley

About the Author

My passion is to empower diverse individuals to unleash their leadership potential, improve decision-making, and reach their desired goals through an innovative coaching partnership to increase growth, satisfaction, success, and resiliency.

We partner together to harness the greatness within you and you'll learn how to lead yourself, others, and your organization/business. Women, in particular, tend to have self-limiting thoughts that keep them from reaching their full potential. That is where I come in to help defeat these thoughts and help my clients overcome the fear that holds them back.

What do I offer?

- ❖ 1:1 and group coaching for individuals who want to set goals, change their lives, and take action towards the life they want.
- ❖ Leadership development courses to help bridge the knowledge gap around leading self, others, and their organization/business.

- ❖ Safe space to fight your inner-critic and create tactics to overcome the self-defeating thoughts from our inner-critic and imposter syndrome.

- ❖ Organization Development (OD), Team development, Board retreats and Retreats

I am certified in the following Coaching arenas:

International Coaching Federation (ICF) Coach at the Professional Certified Coach (PCC) level

- ❖ Certified Executive Coach, CEC
- ❖ Certified Visionary Leadership Coach, CVLC
- ❖ Certified Women Empowerment Coach
- ❖ Certified MentorCoach, CMC
- ❖ Crucial Conversations
- ❖ Emotional Intelligence 2.0 and 360
- ❖ Proci Change Management Practitioner
- ❖ DiSC Instructor
- ❖ Real Colors Facilitator

CONTACT INFORMATION

Mindy Gillis
Mindy's Executive Coaching LLC
www.linkedin.com/in/mindygillis
mindy@mindycoaching.com
904-994-7023

"
"I didn't have anybody, really, no foundation in life, so I had to make my own way. Always, from the start. I had to go out in the world and become strong, to discover my mission in life."

—Tina Turner"

Sallie Wagner

Dedication

I dedicate this to my grandmother, mother, daughter, daughters-in-law, granddaughters, and all the other powerful and courageous women before and after me.

From Regret to resilience with M*S*G™

by Sallie Wagner

Are you successfully discontent like I used to be? Does your life look pretty good on paper yet doesn't feel so good on the inside?

Are you ready to take your life and/or your business to the next level, yet maybe don't quite know what that might be or how to make it happen?

Many years ago, as I asked myself those questions, I realized my life was full of regret, and that regret came from the realization that I was living somebody else's life rather than my own. I was a non-player character in my own life.

When I was a child, I always wanted to be a teacher. In college, I majored in Theology. I started in physics, ended up in meta-physics, and planned to become a professor of Theology.

Then I met my first husband. The first night we met, he said, *"You should be a lawyer."* Guess what? I'm a lawyer.

I spent my career living somebody else's vision for my life.

Fortunately, life conspired to change all of that and I rediscovered my earlier vision for my life of being a teacher.

This time, I listened to the message that life was sending me. I focused on teaching opportunities. When I did that, everything changed, to the point where I had to scale back. Yet, the universe still wasn't done with me—it never is!

Eventually, perhaps a bit reluctantly, I followed the trail of breadcrumbs that led me to life coaching—I became a life strategist to guide people to discover the life that makes them come alive. A life alchemist to guide people to transform their lives and uncover the magic that lies within them.

It was a long journey, yet I still made it. Now, I know that there are steps that would have accelerated that journey for me. I could have taken the shortcut rather than the scenic route.

That's why I've created a protocol to guide you to create, and take, your own shortcut. It will save you time and effort and, perhaps, mistakes along the way.

The first step is to recognize that everything is a choice.

When you understand this truth, you can begin the process. Just take the first step and decide.

Ask yourself, do I want it? Or have I **decided** for it?

Because, you see, wanting isn't the same as deciding. Wanting is magical thinking, wishing and hoping that something will happen. Deciding is wanting **plus** action. Deciding is wanting something so much that you take the necessary steps to make sure it happens. You become the person who does the things it takes to have the life you've decided for yourself.

And that means, moving out of regret. And the best way to move out of regret is to build resilience.

REGRET

We all have regrets in life. Those choices and decisions we made, or didn't make. Those things that make us think, *"If only . . ."*

That's the gut-check definition of regret – does it conjure up one of those "if only" statements?

- ❖ **"If only"** I hadn't done this.
- ❖ **"If only"** I had done that.

241

Seventeen years ago, I was living with regret. My first husband had died. In the early hours of that morning, so many years ago, when I fell into a troubled sleep, I was married. When I woke up, I was a widow.

I felt numb, frozen in the trauma of loss. Yet the numbness was punctuated by knee-buckling pain and grief.

I also felt guilty.

I fell asleep. Maybe if I hadn't fallen asleep, he wouldn't have died.

Days before, he told me how tired he was. I knew what he was telling me. He was too tired to fight anymore. I told him it was okay. If he needed to go, he could go. He asked if the kids would be okay, if I'd be okay. I lied. I told him yes, we would be okay.

In those moments after he died, I really felt, and believed, that somehow I had killed him. **If only** I hadn't given him permission. If I hadn't told him it was okay, he wouldn't have died. **If only** I hadn't fallen asleep. If I hadn't fallen asleep, he wouldn't have died.

If only . . .

As those moments turned into months, all that regret kept me from living my life.

WHOSE LIFE ARE YOU LIVING?

When we're faced with mortality—whether our own or those we love - we start to question our lives.

Bonnie Ware worked for many years with people who were dying. Based on that work, she compiled a list—and she's written extensively—of the top five regrets that people express at the end of their lives.

The most common regret is:

> **"**
> *I wish I'd had the courage to live a life true to myself,*
> *not the life others expected of me.*
> —www.bronnieware.com

As if to say, **if only** I'd had the courage to live the life that makes me come alive. **If only** I'd had the courage to be the main character of my own life, rather than a non-player character.

You see, as people looked back over their lives, with the clarity that comes from facing their own mortality, they realized that they hadn't lived out **their** dreams. And they also realized that it was because of their own choices.

Many of us experience regrets throughout our lives—not only at the end of our lives.

According to Kathy Caprino, one of the top five regrets expressed by mid-career professionals around the world is: I wish I hadn't listened to other people about what I should study and pursue. [https://kathycaprino.com/2016/10/top-5-regrets-mid-career-professionals/]

Again, as if to say, **if only** I had pursued my own passions and my own course of studies. **If only** I had been the main character in my own life.

That sounds remarkably like the top regret of people at the end of life. You see . . . it's not only people who are dying; people at any stage of life, people who are **not living** also experience the same type of regret.

Fortunately, we don't need to wait until the end of life to start living it!

Many people have experienced the phenomenon of Post Traumatic Growth—rather than staying stuck in the trauma of their particular life events, they are propelled into personal growth and understandings that, significantly, mirror the top five regrets of the dying, only in a positive way.

So, rather than regretting that they lived the life that was expected of them, they have a new-found sense of meaning and purpose. They're able to focus on their own goals and dreams, rather than living out the dreams and goals of others. They move from NPC to main character.

Again, fortunately, we don't need to wait until we're faced with traumatic events to experience the wisdom of this awakening.

We can discover and enjoy the benefits of Post-Ecstatic Growth—by undertaking a significant challenge in our lives. For example:

- ❖ training for and participating in an athletic event
- ❖ writing a book
- ❖ starting a business
- ❖ changing a habit
- ❖ embarking on a spiritual journey

So instead of waiting for life to smack you on the head with trauma, you make a preemptive strike by choosing your **own** challenge—you intentionally take on a meaningful project or mission.

M*S*G™

M*S*G™ is your key to deciding on and accepting that challenge of defeating the Alien Overlords of regret and building resilience to become the main character in your own life.

M*S*G™ stands for:

❖ Mindset
❖ Skillset
❖ Get Off Your Asset!

Mindset

Mindset is not just thinking happy thoughts, like Peter Pan.

Mindset is having faith. It is not necessarily religious faith, although it may also be that. Mindset is being courageous enough to confront the facts of your circumstances, and still having faith that you will prevail.

As Jane McGonigal has written, it's easier when you think of it as a game – where you're the hero of the story, and the challenge you've chosen is your quest. [SuperBetter: The Power of Living Gamefully] That is the Mindset you must choose for yourself.

One of the best ways to succeed in your quest is to build resilience in four key areas of life:

- ❖ physical
- ❖ emotional
- ❖ mental
- ❖ social

Skillset

That's where Skillset comes in. Skillset includes new skills and new knowledge of how to change your thinking to have the right Mindset, as well as how to build resilience.

Physical Resilience

Physical resilience is your body's ability to withstand physical challenges, maintain stamina, handle stress, and heal itself when it's damaged or harmed in some way.

You strengthen your physical resilience in 3 major ways:

- ❖ become physically active
- ❖ consume nourishing food, drink, and thoughts

❖ avoid harmful diversions, like substances and binge/re-strict behaviors

If you're already doing these things, well done you! Keep it up!

If not, do something every day—stand up and stretch, walk around the block, treat yourself to a healthful snack, unplug from social media and other distractions.

Emotional Reslience

Emotional resilience is your ability to choose positive emotions on demand. This is your ability to respond, rather than react, to your life circumstances.

You build and strengthen your emotional resilience through:

❖ self-discovery and creative expression
❖ finding and fulfilling a purpose in life
❖ mindfulness

If you're already doing these things, well done you! Keep it up!

If not, do something every day—do something artistic (draw, sing, play music), find and work toward your mission in life, become more mindful by noticing what you're noticing.

Mental Resilience

Mental resilience is your ability to think flexibly, consider alternatives, develop systems and structures with action steps to reach a goal, understand different perspectives, and solve problems using your creativity.

You build and strengthen your mental resilience by:

- ❖ working puzzles and playing games
- ❖ finding new hobbies
- ❖ learning new languages
- ❖ reading new books

Sometimes, this can be challenging, especially for perfectionists. We may be reluctant to try new things because we know we're not going to be good at them.

Here's the remedy for that—give yourself enough grace and time to be bad at something new. That's the only way you'll get good at it!

If you're already doing these things, well done, you! Keep it up!

If not, do something every day—read, learn, play games.

Social Resilience

Social resilience comes through connecting with others in social situations:

- ❖ spending time with friends and/or family
- ❖ working as part of a team
- ❖ getting involved with your community

If you're already doing these things, well done, you! Keep it up!

If not, do something every day—reach out to friends and family, volunteer in your community, join a group.

As you develop resilience in these four areas, you begin to move out of regret. You begin to live out the learnings of Post Traumatic Growth, and Post Ecstatic Growth.

It doesn't take a lot, just consistent action every day. Small steps, every day, will build resilience and courage.

The key is, you have to take action to build resilience, you can't just think about it.

GET OFF YOUR ASSET!

Once you identify your resilience goals, you're ready to take action.

However, be prepared...what comes next is what stops most people before they get started.

As they start to manifest a new Mindset and hone a new Skill-set, they get stopped by fear.

Fear shows up as indecision, distraction, and self-sabotage. Fear is subtle.

It sounds like the voice of reason.

It says things like:

- ❖ How am I going to do that?
- ❖ I've never done that before.
- ❖ Now's not a good time.
- ❖ Should I really be doing this?
- ❖ I can't do that.

Have you heard those voices, or others?

Don't be the person who is pushed by fear. Allow yourself to be pulled by the vision of the life of resilience and courage you're creating for yourself!

It comes down to fear or faith.

You decide.

It's all about deciding and making a commitment to and for yourself.

COMMITMENT

All it takes is 100% commitment.

Anything less than 100%, even 99.999%, is so hard! It is filled with excuses, and reasons, not to take the steps that will lead from regret to resilience and courage.

100% commitment is so easy! There are no excuses or reasons, just doing. You simply need to follow your system every day. Every day, you should move in the direction of your goals.

Commit yourself 100% with my 30-day challenge.

For 30 days, change your Mindset to one of resilience and courage. Maintain the Mindset to see your life as a quest, with you as the main character, the hero of your own journey through life.

For 30 days, develop the Skillset to build resilience and courage by taking those small steps every day.

For 30 days, take action to bring that resilience and courage into the landscape of your reality.

You have to take action to achieve your goals.

The right Mindset and Skillset will empower you to take the right action and make that 100% commitment—to you!

Remember, as Ralph Waldo Emerson said, *"The only person you are destined to become is the person you decide to be."*

Decide for it.

Don't just want it.

Decide for you.

Move from regret to resilience with M*S*G™!

About the Author

SALLIE specializes in helping women reclaim their power over their own lives. She uses Emotional Freedom Techniques (EFT), Evolved Neurolinguistic Programming (eNLP), and trauma-aware modalities so clients launch into action and gain access to rapid, concrete results as they ditch habits, behaviors, fears, phobias, limiting beliefs and decisions that hold them back in life.

Speaker, author, lawyer, real estate broker and instructor, and life coach, Sallie spent the majority of her law career in the corporate world, working in real estate for various industries. She currently owns and operates a company that provides broker and contract compliance services to real estate brokerages throughout Florida. Serving over 2,500 real estate agents, averaging 600 transactions each week, with annual sales volume in excess of $6 Billion, Sallie provides timely assistance to agents on contract questions and transaction pitfalls, facilitating as tens of thousands of families achieve their home ownership dreams.

Sallie also owns and operates a real estate school, providing exceptional educational opportunities for real estate professionals throughout Florida.

CONTACT INFORMATION

Sallie Wagner
Intentional Life Coaching LLC
swagner@salliewagnerenterprises.com
816.616.5403
https://www.linkedin.com/in/sallieintentionallifecoaching/
https://www.facebook.com/SallieColacoWagner
salliewagner.com

Shira Raymond

Dedication

To the Almighty God who gave me the creative inspiration to grow in ways I never thought possible and allowing me to bring my message to the world. And to my children Asher Pesach, Nechama (Natalie) and Bruriah, I wish you all continued success in your lives and to live each day as if it was your last. With Love always!

30 Days to Reclaiming Your Life

THE POWER OF NEW BEGINNINGS

by Shira Raymond

Life is a continuum that evolves every moment of every day. Our choice is how we are going to live. Do you continue the path that you are already on, or are you ready and willing to embrace change? For most people, there is a fear of the unknown or a lack of trust in oneself to dream big and create something different.

Do you have limiting beliefs that are keeping you stuck in the past and blind your abilities to create a different future?

There are times in our lives that change the trajectory forever. Are you ready to create the next chapter of your life on your terms? Life is meant to be embraced, with the idea that everything that happens to us is for our personal growth. It is very rare to find anyone who hasn't experienced some kind of trauma in their lives, whether we were bullied, physically or emotionally assaulted, went through a difficult divorce or loss of a loved one, etc... the list is endless. These events were not meant to cripple you but to empower you to grow so you can fulfill what you were created for.

This is powerful! Every one of you is special and created to make an impact in this world. When you begin to understand that our life has purpose, it should affect the way we look at it. For some, their gifts might be to influence millions of people's lives, and for others it might be to affect the people they are closest to. If we aren't the best versions of ourselves, how are we going to inspire change in others?

Let me tell you a little about myself. I was the middle child of three sisters and sandwiched between a CPA and an Attorney. I struggled with a learning disability in the way I process language. As you can imagine, school was always a struggle for me, until my early thirties when I decided to go back to college. At college, I was finally evaluated, and learned the skills to conquer my learning limitations. Needless-to-say this affected my self-esteem, since I always felt I was a disappointment to my mother. I constantly heard *"she's not trying hard enough"* or *"she's not smart enough."* When you hear these things enough, you absorb them. Add being bullied in school and other incidents of physical and emotional abuse—life was tough. I didn't love myself, nor did I feel lovable.

I became a person that embraced change. I was always in search of personal growth because the past was too painful. I knew there was a better life for me. I just needed to find the secret to my own happiness.

I was blessed to go back to school about 10 years ago and received a degree in Mind, Body Transformational Psychology. This is when my personal growth went to a new level. I realized that I do not need to rehash every negative event in my life to create happiness. Everything I needed was within me! I just needed to change my perspective on life and begin living in gratitude. Gratitude is one of the most powerful tools out there, and all you need to do is embrace it.

Living in gratitude means truly being grateful for all the events in your life, and understanding that each moment has a purpose for your higher good. It also means that you need to stop blaming everyone or anything that might have "harmed or hurt" you in the past. When we stop blaming others, we unclip our wings and can begin to soar.

This is the part where most people get stuck. When we blame others, we choose not to take personal responsibility for our lives. We give our power to others. An example of this could be a woman who was physically assaulted when she was younger.

She could blame the assailant for her emotional and physical well being. How does this mentality serve you? What if you were in a marriage for 15, 20 or 30 years to someone who was emotionally damaged, and your marriage was a wreck. How does it help you to blame them for the state of your marriage when you decided to stay in it anyway? I recently asked my husband of 24 years for a divorce. The bottom line was I grew to live in gratitude, and he chose not to. I realized that if I stayed, I would never be happy and always feel pulled down emotionally. If I wanted to, I could blame him for his lack of growth that ended our marriage or look at the experience with gratitude. I choose the latter. In fact, recently I told him that I have no hard feelings. I feel blessed that I was able to grow into the person I am today because I was married to him.

Are you ready to reclaim your life today? Are you ready to take 100% responsibility for every aspect of your life? Do you have the tenacity to create the future you have always dreamed of (or are ready to dream about) on your terms? We have all heard the term *"what we think about grows."* When we focus on the negative things in our lives that is what we see more of. God or Universe will always show us more of that. The amazing thing is this is true for "gratitude." I have seen it in my own life. The more I see the good in every situation or in the people I meet, the more people, situations, or things show up in my life for me to be grateful about. So which side of the spectrum do you want to be on? For me, I love the miracles. What would you choose?

As children we have great imaginations and, at some point in our life, we switch that off as if it isn't an adult thing to do. I would like to challenge that idea. The most successful people in the world use their imagination to create every aspect of their life, whether it be their personal or professional life. Ellen Sirleaf says, *"If your dreams don't scare you, they're not big enough."* Who is stopping you from dreaming big and creating your life on your terms? Taking 100% responsibility for all your life choices is empowering. Do you have the courage to do that?

Over the next month I would like to encourage you to begin the process of reclaiming your life and begin to shift your perspective on what you can achieve in your life. Each week you will be challenged with exercises to break free from the past and become clear about what you would like your life to look like.

THE FIRST WEEK I would like you to spend a minimum of 10 minutes a day daydreaming about the life you would like to create if there were no obstacles in your way. I don't want you to think about, or worry about, if it could become a reality. I want you to dream so big that if you shared your dreams with others, they would think you might be crazy. Each day dream about a different aspect of your life and make sure you journal your results as you will need them for next week's activity.

Things to dream about: if you're single and looking for a relationship what would that look like? If you're married and your marriage needs work, what would your marriage look like? Where would you like to live if money wasn't an issue? What would your dream house look like? How much money would you like in your bank account? What would you like your physical health to be like? Would you like to travel? What would be on your bucket list of things you would like to do in your life? The point here is to go BIG! Share them in my Facebook group so we can encourage and empower your dreams to reality at: https://www.facebook.com/groups/239475697586303

WEEK TWO: create a vision board using words or pictures so you have a physical image of all the areas of your life that you dreamed about last week. Buy a piece of poster board or create it on the web. Find pictures on the internet or in magazines. This should include a picture of a dream house, job, the perfect relationship, how much money you would have, what would you do for fun... Begin by laying out all your pictures on your board before you glue them down so you can move them around or add/cut as needed. Once you have completed your vision board, take a picture and upload it in the Facebook group as well as hang it up in a place where you will look at it several times a day.

WEEK THREE is where you begin to internalize your vision and begin to live as if you already have those things in your life. The purpose of this is to reprogram your subconscious mind for the lifestyle you want to create. Don't let the limiting beliefs hold you back from creating your dream life. We know through quantum physics that everything in this world is made up of energy and vibration. Did you know that this includes your thoughts and emotions as well? What you think about grows, so if you want to make a change in your circumstances you need to change your thoughts around them. Like attracts like.

Change your emotional vibration and you begin to attract more positive things into your life. This can be challenging at the beginning when you are trying to imagine yourself living in your dream house and still coming home to your much smaller house. One of the ways to get around this is to tell yourself that the house you are living in right now is a temporary house while your dream house is being built. Don't forget to be thankful for all these wonderful things that are on your list. Take a few minutes daily to close your eyes and envision your future life as if it is happening now. How would you feel? What can you smell, see, feel, taste and hear? The more senses you can attribute to this vision, the more real it will become.

WEEK FOUR consists of raising your emotional vibration so you can attract the life you dream about today. The first thing that I want you to do is to make a list of 5 things you are grateful for. You may think this is a crazy amount, but it is much easier than you think when you first look at all the things you take for granted. Let me get you started: you have eyes to see, ears to hear, a mouth to taste, teeth to chew, hands to touch, legs to take you from one place to the next, feet to stand on, a heart that beats without effort, a roof over your head, family or friends to support you. These are your first ten things. Get creative and have fun with this activity. It is the most important activity you will do because this exercise will raise your vibration to allow you to attract the things into your life that you desire. Once you have your list, I want you to review it every morning when you wake and right before you go to sleep at night. This will begin to program your mind for gratitude. Next, carry a copy with you and whenever you find yourself in those old negative thought patterns, pull out your list and read it. The more you do this, the faster you will shift your mindset from negative to living in gratitude. When you live in gratitude, you see every event in your life as a blessing and can be thankful for the bad as well as the good.

The more you put this into practice the faster you will find a shift in your mindset. In a short period of time, you will find yourself in the positive states instead of the negative and when the negative thoughts come in, you can now bless and release them.

About the Author

SHIRA RAYMOND is a leader in the life transformation field for women, who are ready to begin their personal journey to empowerment. Her coaching encompasses all three aspects of emotionally, physically and spiritually. Shira teaches women how to master their mindset and emotions, empowering them to grow in ways they never thought possible. She is the CEO Shira Raymond Coaching and Women's Empowerment International. She has two books coming out the first half of 2022. Her mission: Create the next chapter of your life, on your terms.

Shira became obsessed with self-help and personal development in her mid-twenties. Though her own life, and recent divorce, she understood that it her duty to help women create a positive loving relationship with themselves, God and others. Her coaching empowers woman on how to master their mindset and emotions so that they can profoundly change every aspect of their lives with no regrets.

She realized after raising her kids and ending her marriage of 24 years that she could embrace the next chapter of her life with strength and dignity to create the type of life she always dreamed about.

CONTACT INFORMATION:

Shira Raymond
www.shiraraymond.com
ebook: Embrace New Beginnings

"

"Peace cannot exist without justice, justice cannot exist without fairness, fairness cannot exist without development, development cannot exist without democracy, democracy cannot exist without respect for the identity and worth of cultures and peoples."

—Rigoberta Menchú

Simone Sloan

Dedication

This chapter is dedicated to Joshua and Violet Sloan.

Lean, Learn, and Elevate

ENHANCING YOUR DEI JOURNEY

by Simone Sloan

Inclusion is striving to avoid treating others as part of a mysterious suspect, or as generic representatives of a larger group, rather than as individuals. Inclusion is making people feel they are respected and valued; that they belong.

Inclusion is a choice. It takes a lot of effort. It requires being intentional in our self-awareness and reflection; consistently re-evaluating our perspectives, experiences, and journeys. It also requires the courage to leave our comfort zone.

Greg was a U.S. business consultant struggling to find the courage to leave his comfort zone. He felt badly when he saw people being excluded; ideas ignored at meetings, missing out on career-building projects, passed over for mentoring opportunities. Yet, he wouldn't speak up even knowing that his silence offered tacit approval of exclusive behavior.

He wanted to be more comfortable with conversations about race but feared the criticism he would receive for going against the grain. And he worried he might say the wrong thing and appear bumbling and clueless. To become more vocal and inclusive, Greg would have to lean hard into his discomfort.

Wherever you are in your diversity, equity, and inclusion journey, over the next 30 days, you'll be stepping out of your comfort zone in order to become an active participant in displaying inclusion. Stepping out of your comfort zone isn't easy, but we encourage you to push through your fear to reach a place of learning and growth. You are being asked to read and listen to other voices, create a plan of action, and develop an accountability system to keep you moving out of your default routines and patterns. It will be worth it.

Remember that diversity alone does not equal inclusion. Many companies have focused on diversity. The McKinsey study, *"Diversity Wins: How Inclusion Matters"* found that industries such as financial services, technology, and healthcare showed a 52% positive sentiment towards diversity but a much lower 29% positive sentiment on inclusion. But hiring diverse talent does not in itself create an inclusive environment. Inclusion requires treating people in a way that gives them a sense of belonging and allows them to thrive. This is determined in part by the workplace environment, experiences, and practices. Each of us has the power to make our environment feel more or less inclusive.

Inclusion benefits everyone. Businesses gain wider perspectives and a deeper talent pool, people widen their social world and open up new experiences, and all of society becomes stronger and more varied.

FIRST ASSIGNMENT: DEFINE YOUR COMFORT ZONE

Take a piece of paper and divide it into 3 columns labeled "comfort," "fear," and "action."

Now put each of these actions in the comfort or fear column:

- ❖ Speaking up when someone misrepresents a subject, situation, person, etc.
- ❖ Challenging misstatements by those above you at work.
- ❖ Actively trying to include those being excluded.
- ❖ Bringing up exclusionary practices you see with peers.
- ❖ Talking about diversity and culture with people.
- ❖ Admitting you don't know something at the risk of seeming stupid or uninformed.
- ❖ Going against the grain.

❖ Risking negative repercussions in order to take a positive stand.

Look at the items in the fear column. Think about what you can do to move them to comfort. Which items would you start first? Discuss and share your list with a trusted friend or colleague, and share strategies with them. Actively practice a mindset of worrying less about what other people think.

Over the next month, you'll explore biases, find new ways to communicate, explore cultural differences, and learn how to respond with empathy. Ultimately, you'll find ways to be more inclusive, and find the courage to push for more inclusion among others at home and work.

As you increase your awareness of yourself and the world around you over the next 30 days, take a few minutes each day to reflect on and describe what you've learned or observed. The form of this description is up to you: you can journal, record a short video, post on social media, or make art—whatever is meaningful to you. Share these with others or keep them to yourself; this is your journey.

WEEK ONE: CONSCIOUS AND UNCONSCIOUS BIAS

Monique, a global manager, was scared to make her first visit to Russia, having absorbed a lifetime of stereotypes about the country. She thought that it would not be US-friendly nor welcoming. But the Russia she entered was unexpected, with more enthusiasm for religion, US culture, capitalism, and American cars than she had believed. Instead of a country populated with a strange and foreign "them," she found Russia full of people not unlike her friends and neighbors. If she was wrong about Russians, she thought, perhaps she had wrong assumptions about other groups as well?

We all have biases that come out of our experiences and beliefs. Some are conscious, like distrusting people with different political or religious beliefs, while others are subconscious; we react differently to certain people without even realizing why.

These biases affect many of our decisions: who we befriend, who we work with, and who we avoid.

Assignment: Learn your biases

TO DO: The Implicit Association Test explores an individual's unconscious bias in search of subconscious associations of certain racial, cultural, gender, or other groups with particular concepts. Go to https://implicit.harvard.edu/implicit/takeatest. html and take a few tests. If they reveal a difference between your conscious beliefs and behaviors, ask yourself what different choices you might have made in your life without these underlying biases.

TO OBSERVE: This week, question your biases. Pay attention to how you react and respond to every person. Do you stand nearer or further away? Smile or frown? Would you feel and act the same if they were of a different culture, gender, sexual orientation, or ethnicity?

WEEK TWO: INCLUSIVE COMMUNICATION

Miquel, a CEO in the financial services sector, asked me to uncover why people across his organization couldn't communicate with each other. Over a series of conversations with his employees, I discovered that they simply did not feel safe. 2SLGBTQIA+ groups reported negative comments circulating during the first work-time celebration of PRIDE. Biracial, Black, Indigenous, People of Colour (BIPOC) female professionals saw their managers push back when they were proactive about their careers. Even the all-male senior leadership team felt scared to challenge the CEO.

Miquel was confused and heartbroken. He had asked for feedback and attempted to create opportunities to share differences. What went wrong?

What you say and how it is said matters. Miquel needed to look not just at the words he used but his non-verbal communication. When your tone and body language indicate that negative feedback upsets you, asking for feedback won't create open communication. If Miquel could align his verbal and non-verbal approach, he could foster an inclusive environment that ran throughout the company.

Communication is important to ensure people feel heard and included. When that communication is wanting, people keep secrets, our words are used against us, and it feels unsafe to offer opinions or critiques.

Assignment: Observe your communication

This week, try to be conscious of your language and increase its inclusivity.

- ❖ Introduce yourself by including your pronouns.
- ❖ Instead of referring to someone's "girlfriend" or "husband," use "partner."

- ❖ Avoid gendered pronouns, like "guys", "chairman", and "manpower."

- ❖ Adapt your language to the listener—consider their needs, values, and interests.

- ❖ Ask questions with genuine curiosity.

- ❖ Listen actively, check to make sure you understand what they are saying and ask follow-up questions.

- ❖ To create an environment that ensures people feel psychologically safe when providing feedback, by spotting, explaining, and appreciating their strengths.

- ❖ When someone makes a negative statement toward different cultures, ethnicity, gender, abilities, religion, sexual orientation, or race, speak out.

WEEK THREE: CULTURAL DIFFERENCES

Alex and Juan had lived across from each other in a Miami Highrise for over ten years. When they saw each other, they would stand in their doorways talking about weather and sports. Their doors were open, each with an arm stretched across the way, a perhaps unconscious symbol of the limits of their acquaintanceship.

Either could have stepped aside to say, *"come in, let's get to know each other better."* Either would have entered if invited. But neither felt comfortable taking the initiative.

We tend to gravitate towards those we see as most like us, from a similar culture, gender, ethnicity, education level, etc. When we see a different appearance or hear an accent, many times our curiosity turns off.

People, like icebergs, show only a little on the surface. Values, skills, unique and special qualities, require a deeper dive. By consciously or unconsciously dismissing certain people as the "other" you are choosing exclusion and losing out on amazing connections and deeper understanding of others.

Assignment: Expand your world

TO READ: What is Othering?

TO DO: List your characteristics—gender, sexual orientation, religion, income level, political party. Now do it for those you know well. Is there wide variety, or narrow similarity?

TO EXPLORE: Learn about another culture, one outside of your day-to-day experience. Try the food, listen to the music, read up on the culture (preferably books by members of that culture), learn some of the language. If you meet people from that culture, ask them something you're curious about. Ask with sensitivity, using phrases like *"I'm really curious about* _____ and I'm wondering if you can help me," or "I'm interested in what you think about _____."

WEEK 4: EMPATHY

"I am a great doctor," Carl told me. "So, what's the problem?"

A talented surgeon, Carl was very well-liked by his patients and very disliked by co-workers, who found him mean and ego-driven. Employee attrition and absence rates were high on his team.

Carl thought of himself as empathetic, but staff feedback suggested otherwise. As we worked together, I introduced empathy as part of his coaching. He began to practice the three levels of empathy: cognitive (understanding others' perspective), emotional (feeling others' feelings), and concern (sensing others' needs). Carl realized his title and gender came with privileges that he was using dictatorially, ignoring staff input, centering himself in every conversation, and, in the process, driving away talent.

As he started to realize the negative impact he was having on his staff, he started listening more, asking for feedback and allowing others to lead in conversations and have a say in their working conditions. This was how he began to learn how to earn the trust of those around him.

As Carl began to consistently empathize with the staff, they began to feel respected, seeing themselves as valued stake-holders in a company where everyone matters. An important key to inclusion, then, is empathy. A study, *"Perspective Taking Combats Automatic Expressions of Racial Bias,"* indicated that putting yourself in someone else's shoes can lessen racist atti-tudes by reducing unconscious bias.

Karla McLaren, author of The Art of Empathy, says empathy is an inherent human trait. But if others find you unempathetic it's a sign that you need to work more to cultivate your natural empathy.

Assignment: Practice empathy

TO-DO: Take McLaren's empathy test (https://karlamclaren. com/are-you-an-empath/).

SELF-AWARENESS CHALLENGE: Be curious about yourself. How much do you talk versus listen? How are you being received and perceived by others? Are people eager to talk to you or do

---

they seem to avoid you? If you were them, would you want to be treated the way you treat them?

Obtain feedback, either in the moment or after the interaction. You can ask others if your language was too harsh. You could also ask if there was a better way to approach a topic. However, if your body language says you don't want to know, no one will tell you.

SPEAK WITH INTENTION: Have a strategy in mind before interacting with others. Think about your approach, cadence, and word choices. Put yourself in the other person's shoes and think about what is important to them. Consider how what you intend to say will feel to the other person. While speaking to them, observe their words and body language as guides to what they're feeling, and adapt your language if they seem to be reacting negatively or positively.

THE FINAL DAY: KEEP GOING

It takes work to be truly inclusive in your life. Old patterns are difficult to escape, so keep a watchful eye on your attitudes and actions to avoid old patterns.

Our biases and assumptions keep us from seeing people fully. Staying aware of these biases and challenging our assumptions keeps us from dividing people into "us" and "them."

ASSIGNMENT: Continue to focus on inclusion and the impact on others. Constantly challenge your assumptions, observe your behaviors, and continue to grow. Connect with me at www. YourChoiceCoach.com and share your inclusive journey with me.

About the Author

SIMONE SLOAN is the founder of Your Choice Coach, an executive coaching and diversity, equity, and inclusion consulting firm.

CONTACT INFORMATION

Simone Sloan
Your Choice Coach
www.YourChoiceCoach.com
info@yourchoicecoach.com
https://www.linkedin.com/in/simonesloan/
https://www.facebook.com/simone.sloan.526/

Siobhan Cunningham

Dedication

To my daughters and courageous sisters who served in the military.

Stop Playing Nice! You're A Badass Lady

SIOBHAN'S STORY

by Siobhan Cunningham

DO YOU REMEMBER THE HEYDAYS OF YOUR YOUTH?

In my 20s, my professional career was on fire, and my life rotated around having exciting experiences! I was climbing the corporate ladder and feeling quite confident about my ability to accomplish whatever goal I set for myself. At that time, each accomplishment was a glimpse into approval that I desperately needed. A little praise was the dopamine fuel that kept me checking-off the adulting boxes. I had a close-knit circle of sister-friends, and Ne-Yo's "Ms. Independent" was my unofficial theme song. At 29, I believed I reached my career peak and was ready for a new career challenge.

It wasn't entirely out of character for me to decide to join the US Air Force as a Social Work Officer. No one told me that 5 years is a long commitment for someone to have little control over their life, especially when you are used to being lucky enough to make quick and successful career moves. At least in the military, I had financial and medical stability. Once I transitioned into being a veteran, I struggled with knowing my place in the world.

I was secretly terrified that if I failed at another career goal, I'd lose the support of my loved ones. The pressure to make money by helping others in a way that illuminates my heart and soul was getting further out of my reach. No one would take me seriously after I failed at my military career.

Have you ever tried to hide your failures?

If you asked me when I was fresh out of the service, I'd say the military was my breaking point. The ultimate failure. I chose to leave my 5 year commitment a year early for the sake of my sanity. Surprisingly, my burnout and anger peaked once I was out of the military. I found myself underemployed, newly married, and expecting my first child, still figuring out what authenticity means to me. Being the good girl who works hard and follows the rules wasn't working anymore.

It was time to create a business that showcased my knowledge in meaningful ways.

Imagine how defeating it is going into a new role or business venture with your failures taunting you in the middle of the night. Now, think about not having a safe space to share how your experiences changed you. Some people are afraid of how other people will judge them. Others don't want to be disowned or disloyal to their service in the community. It can make you feel alone.

It's time to create a business that showcases your knowledge and passion in meaningful ways.

USE WHAT YOU'VE TRIED TO CREATE WHAT WORKS FOR YOU

It's hard to have fun when you're stuck in the downward spiral of not knowing what you want to do with your life. You dream about finally having the spare time and freedom to pursue your wildest dreams. Yet, you find yourself wasting time because you have the energy all of the sudden. This crippling lack of focus happens when there's a disconnect between your passion and your actions. Not having a well-laid-out plan with tangible goals will cost you emotionally and financially.

What have you already tried?

First, take a moment to acknowledge the investment you've already made into your future goals. Close your eyes and lovingly reflect on the lessons learned from each setback or failure. If you've eagerly joined special interest groups and professional networking memberships to help you meet people you could collaborate with in the future, or listened to all the podcasts and completed all the group coaching programs from your favorite famous multimillion-dollar coaches. There was a moment or two when you regretted moving on your instincts.

Honor that feeling. Believe that those moments of regret are simple reminders that you haven't finished learning and you're on a journey. People with stressful and highly regimented careers (such as the military or being a caregiver) become exceptional at planning and predicting every worst-case scenario.

The belief that failure is not an option leaves little room for creativity and growth. If defeat equals not planning hard enough or not doing enough, then it's easy to connect failure to not being good enough.

Have you considered how your heart feels?

Often, the answer is, "not really...."

It's easy to find coaching services from your favorite gurus to help simplify the complexities of your problems. After putting that advice into practice, it's clear that those shallow solutions only offer pieces of the puzzle. In other words, very logical solutions to emotional roadblocks.

Start confronting emotional roadblocks. Notice if your mindset is in fixed or growth mode. When strategizing your next steps, use insights from those disappointing experiences. Success does not fall solely on your ability to perform. There isn't a fixed path to success. Eventually, your greatest insecurities and frustrations will stand between you and your next-level-self.

Now is the time to tap into the past experiences that made you feel invisible or dismissed. Consider doing this in imaginative ways. A fixed mindset is perfect for pinpointing milestones, but the growth mindset allows for the seemingly impossible to happen. You need both skills to thrive.

SIOBHAN'S BREAKING BADDIE STORY

Secretly, I just wanted to be happy no matter what life threw my way. But instead, everything just felt like an exhausting chore. One failed business launch after another, I felt the pressure to make everyone proud. My faith dwindled as my bank account depleted with little financial return on my investments. I was spiraling into a pit of desperation and depression.

While in the USAF, it seemed as if everyone questioned my expertise. After four years of feeling inferior, I believed that I wasn't smart enough to be respected as a leader. The politics of the job was no longer worth the paycheck. I knew that my skills were better utilized through direct service to my kind of people.

Of course, I still was unclear of my new purpose after service, but my military family assured me that I wasn't a worthless failure. The small but mighty support system may not have fully understood my journey, but they were consistently there for me (no matter how crazy I acted). The time and energy that I spent finding the perfect solutions to the wrong problems slowed down my progress. I knew I was on the right track, but nothing ever felt like the next best step for what I wanted to do and who I wanted to serve. I kept asking myself, *"What am I doing wrong?"*

Finally, my heart led me to the truth. I was afraid to fail again. It was time for me to confront the most uncomfortable feelings about myself. At that moment, I stopped being the good girl who puts others before herself and started being a badass lady who handles adulting like a boss. My Breaking Baddie moment. The moment I stopped caring about what people would think of me and leaned into the possibilities of learning from failure to pursue the lifestyle of my dreams.

THE BREAKING BADDIE METHOD

New habits require patience to develop. The Breaking Baddie Method eliminates the drama from managing your schedule by using insightful structure to create focus and flexibility.

1. Get Clear on Your Most Bankable Assets

If you enjoy absorbing information, then that is a bankable skill. The certifications and degrees that you've earned are external validation methods. Pull out the things you love about learning and take inventory of how you manage projects in your life. Don't worry about proving how smart you are because who you are will radiate to the world and organically connect you with your people.

AWARENESS—If you're hazy about where you stand, it's tough to know where you're headed. Before mapping out the trip, embrace what led you to this moment in your journey.

2. *Honor Your Setbacks and Failures*

Passionate people are fueled by the thrill of making a difference in the world in a uniquely meaningful way. Have you noticed yourself pivoting within your business often? Hesitation to stick to the plan after one or two setbacks might connect to fear. Navigating life's challenges create opportunities for growth. While the degree of severity varies, so does the ability to bounce back. Failure does not equal defeat. Start finding small ways to honor your circumstances without diminishing your worth.

FROM DIVA TO BADDIE—What do Lady Gaga, Beyonce, and Mariah Carey have in common? They have a Diva persona. There's nothing wrong with being a diva from time to time. In fact, that level of dedication to your craft is fabulous when used correctly. When it comes to navigating roadblocks, the diva knocks over barriers without much thought of the consequences. While the good girl stops and researches ways to detour without pissing anyone off or getting into trouble, the Baddie takes the time to listen to her intuition and plan with her passion and happiness in mind.

3. Dream with Intention

To create the business of your dreams, you must dream with intention. As your confidence builds from being aware of your strengths and exploring the roadblocks ahead, you can start turning possibilities into strategy. The alignment between your passion-driven business and lifestyle only lasts if it's doable for you. Use the Breaking Baddie Challenge to hone in on your intentions and commit to making moves one step at a time.

THE BREAKING BADDIE CHALLENGE

Let's face it. Your life doesn't just slow down because you decided to start an online business. Your life may seem more jammed packed now that you are in charge of your own money-making adventures. By following this flexible 7-day cycle, you will find the time to get the right things done that will propel you toward success!

Over the next 4 weeks, you are encouraged to plan one goal for each week.

HOW IT WORKS

Prepare

❖ At the close of the busy week, set a timer for 20 mins and sit down with your planner.

Aware

❖ Spend about 5 minutes reflecting on how you feel about the things you've accomplished last week.
❖ Use your mood to help gauge the energy and effort you'll need to put toward your planning decisions.

Affirm

❖ Then, 5 more minutes choosing a word, sentence, or quote that embodies how you want to feel over the current week.
❖ Set your intention for your weekly goal by choosing a mantra or affirmation that supports how you want to feel throughout the week.

Aim

❖ Use the remaining time to pinpoint the most important task you can accomplish in 3 or 4 days. Then, create an itemized checklist of the steps you can finish in one-hour sprints.

❖ It's time to make your goal and put it on your calendar over the next 4 to 5 days.

❖ This method leaves room for you to move things around when life gets in the way of your well thought out plans.

Plug-it In

❖ Think of when you have the most energy and a pocket of quiet time during your days. Squeeze in the easy-to-complete in an hour step into that block of time.

PRO TIP: Set reminders in your online scheduler and your written planner.

THE BADDIE STRATEGY IN ACTION

Day 1: Friday

9:30 PM - Weekly Planning Session (after the kids go to bed)

GOAL: Start a Facebook Community to support my online business.

Day 2: Saturday

8:30 AM - Go into the Breaking Baddie FB Group and ask if anyone wants to be accountability buddies. DM 3 friends who may be interested in being accountability buddies.

Day 3: Sunday

6:00 PM - Create a business page on facebook and start inviting friends to like the page.

Day 4: Monday

Relax

Day 5: Tuesday

10:00 PM - Create a FB group that's linked to my business page and start welcoming new members.

Day 6: Wednesday

Catch-up/Relax

Day 7: Thursday

Catch-up/Relax

About the Author

She's a licensed therapist, US Air Force veteran, wife, mother, and launch strategist. Siobhan is dedicated to helping badass ladies, or Baddies, create the purpose aligned online business of their dreams. Siobhan has been serving clients for 15 years by using her mental health and heart-centered leadership skills to help the women who serve others before themselves using her Baddie Strategy approach.

CONTACT INFORMATION

Siobhan DeAnn LLC
siobhandg@yahoo.com
http://linkedin.com/in/siobhandeann
Facebook.com/siobhandeann
siobhandeann.com

Stacey Hall

Dedication

I dedicate this book to everyone who will use these tips to unleash their inner daredevil and live life fully!

You Will Find Your Courage in Your Comfort Zone

by Stacey Hall

How many times in your life have you been told to "get out of your comfort zone" if you want to be successful?

Were you able to get out of your comfort zone?

Did you stretch yourself without breaking down?

Let's face it... we have all done our best to "get out of our comfort zone" to try to be successful doing something others have told us we "should" do.

And every once in a while, with enough training and support, we find a way to actually do it.

And if we are lucky, we find we actually enjoy it.

I believe when we reach that point, it is only because we simply found a way to expand our comfort zone. We did not actually go beyond it or get out of it.

Many behavior therapists and psychologists agree.

If you are like most people, your mind may already be telling you I am wrong. That "everyone knows" that getting out of our comfort zone is the only way to grow.

I have heard it all before.

I have also heard of the "fight or flight response." How about you?

FIGHT OR FLIGHT?

The fight-or-flight response (also known as the acute stress response), refers to a physiological reaction that occurs when we are in the presence of something that is mentally or physically terrifying.

https://www.verywellmind.com/what-is-the-fight-or-flight-response-2795194

This response is triggered by the release of hormones that prepare your body to either stay and deal with a threat or to run away and get to safety.

Common negative effects on the body and mind caused by the "fight or flight response" to stress and fear are:

1. Increased heart rate and blood pressure

2. Pale or flushed skin—you could be feeling cold and clammy or hot and sweaty

3. Feeling "on edge"—your senses are heightened; you feel you are on guard

4. Memory can be foggy or altered

5. Loss of bowel control

Can you remember feeling this way at any time in your life? Did you feel your heartbeat quicken, did you start breathing faster, and did your entire body become tense?

If you were in danger at the time, then this response was healthy and it allowed you to make sure you found a way to stay safe.

But, if you experienced these symptoms over something that was simply causing you stress—like attempting to do something you had never done before to "get out of your comfort zone"—then you probably got stopped in your tracks... unable to move past the situation, preventing you from achieving other goals.

That is damaging enough, but did you know that frequent activation of the "fight or flight response" is known to cause a range of clinical conditions, including most anxiety disorders?

Debbie Mandel, author of *Addicted to Stress: A Woman's 7 Step Program to Reclaim Joy and Spontaneity in Life* describes the problem this way, *"Many of us are busy escaping from the deficits of our personality by trying to be something we're not. Unfortunately, trying to change your nature—especially in big and bold ways-causes stress: Stress is so inflammatory and it's become the cause of all disease. It zaps energy, creativity, and sabotages relationships."*

Forgive me, but I personally don't think any of these responses to stress and fear will result in greater confidence and courage to achieve our goals.

Do you?

FEAR IS A WARNING SIGN

Going back to the experience that caused you to feel extreme stress, you may remember that you began to feel you were "getting bent out of shape" by attempting to do what would be required to be successful.

You probably felt anxious and worried, which is what caused you to slow down—you were fearful about what was ahead if you continued in this direction.

Fear is what other people tell you to face to be successful. Facing fear and doing whatever it is anyway is supposed to be a sign of courage.

I don't say that. I say fear is an indication that something about what lies ahead is outside of our comfort zone—that we cannot see a way to remain in alignment with our core values and priorities. Fear tells us to check in with ourselves to make sure what we are moving towards is in alignment with our values and purpose.

And if we discover that moving forward feels painful, we can trust that to go further in this direction is to "get out of our own comfort zone." If we attempt to ignore and push past those feelings, we will reach our "breaking point."

That is the point at which we feel we are under constant stress. We have lost our personal power. We feel brittle and we often snap and become useless to ourselves and others—much like a rubber band that has been stretched too far.

CONFIDENCE CONTRIBUTES TO COURAGE

Mental health experts agree that the feeling of confidence improves our mental well-being and produces these benefits:

1. Managing stress and anxiety

2. Influencing others

3. Increasing productivity and creativity

4. Feeling valued

5. Increasing motivation

Now, these sound like factors which actually contribute to success!

And there are physical benefits too, such as:

1. Improved sleep, which contributes to all other physical benefits

2. Improved digestion (no more "eating our gut out" with worries)

3. Strengthened immune system (again, this means increased productivity)

4. Longer lifespan (and the desire to live and be productive longer)

As an example of increasing confidence to strengthen courage, I often hear from my new clients that they have struggled for years attempting to adapt to other people's suggestions of how to be or how they should act.

The stress produced by the desire to please other people weakens their own self-confidence and translates into fear of being themselves.

I encourage them in various ways to take control of their own life by identifying the circumference of their comfort zone.

I explain that the boundaries of their comfort zone are their "core values."

IDENTIFYING THE CIRCUMFERENCE OF YOUR COMFORT ZONE

Our comfort zone, as stated previously, is formed by our core values.

As we grow, personally and professionally, take safe risks, and become more courageous in various situations, our extended comfort zone also grows. Within our comfort zone, we feel connected to, and in alignment with, our core values. This alignment creates the confidence from which to pursue our dreams.

That confidence allows for more freedom of choice in how to keep growing and improving our skills in alignment with our core values.

Growth is much easier because we feel "born to do it"—whatever the "it" is.

Take a moment now to think about a time when you wanted to learn how to do something you had never done before ... maybe play a new instrument, write a book, quilt a blanket, grow your audience on a social media platform, for example ... and you enjoyed the process.

You felt the "why" of what you were doing. You felt aligned with your Purpose and calling as you grew into mastery of new skills and abilities. You could say "it just felt right" to expand in this way!

Now, take another moment, and consider a time when you felt you "should" learn how to do something you had never done before. This would be a time when you procrastinated getting started. Perhaps you never fully mastered the new activity or skill because you could not see the point in moving forward towards its completion.

You may still be wondering why you never finished what you started. Perhaps beating yourself up for not finishing it success-fully? Perhaps feeling that you "chickened out" in some way and that is why you didn't see it through to the end?

Then this may come as good news to you.

What you discovered is that to move forward would have meant being out of alignment with your core values in some way.

Congratulations! You found the edge of your comfort zone.

A LIST OF COMMON CORE VALUES

To strengthen your self-confidence and courage in 30 days or less, I have provided a list here of the most common core val-ues.

As you read through the list, ask yourself:

1. Which of these core values are my top three?
2. Which core value is my #1 MOST IMPORTANT core value?
3. Which core value on this list is the Least Important to me?
4. Are any of my core values missing from this list? (If so, add them to the list.)

These questions have been designed to help you discover the circumference of your own comfort zone—to ensure that you know the core values that are most important to you so you can make choices that are in alignment with these values and strengthen your courage to achieve your goals.

Core Values

- Loyalty
- Consistency
- Optimism
- Spirituality
- Honesty
- Reliability
- Motivated
- Compassion
- Productive
- Generosity
- Open-Mindedness
- Sense of humor
- Wealth
- Personal Growth
- Service
- Health
- Collaboration
- Creativity
- Adventurous
- Authenticity
- Fearlessness
- Trustworthiness
- Kindness
- Respect
- Charity
- Joy
- Social Responsibility
- Animal Care
- Environmental Care
- Equality
- Freedom
- Leadership
- Self-Accountability
- Flexibility
- Friendship
- Justice
- Efficiency
- Responsibility
- Faith
- Transparency
- Diversity
- Fun
- Cooperation

THE SOURCE OF YOUR COURAGE

It is the source of your self-confidence and self-assurance. With this list consciously in your mind and heart, you will feel in control of your life because you accept and trust that you know the direction in which to move forward. From this list you will draw courage and the motivation to slowly and gently e-x-p-a-n-d your comfort zone to achieve ever larger personal and business goals.

In the meantime, because you now know the order of importance of your core values ... you can consciously make choices in any situation to stay true to yourself and maintain alignment within yourself ... even while gently stretching to acquire new skills and experiences you choose to acquire.

You will also quickly know when you feel out-of-alignment.

When you notice you are being asked to stretch in a new way that feels uncomfortable or dangerous, it will be a signal to check in with your core values.

Do you want to expand your comfort zone by stretching in this way?

Or would this stretch take you beyond your comfort zone and to your breaking point?

Either way, you now have a way to control how much you stretch at any given time. That control translates into personal power. And this personal power makes it possible for you to feel confident and courageous in fulfilling your goals from the safety and security of your comfort zone.

I offer the following additional tools to strengthen your self-confidence and courage:

❖ **HOW TO SCHEDULE FOR SUCCESS**: Download at https://ditchyourgrind.gopages.co/SchedulingforSuccess

❖ **HOW TO KICK YOUR MOTIVATION INTO HIGH GEAR E-BOOK**: Download at https://ditchyourgrind.gopages.co/motivation-into-high-gear

❖ **HOW TO TRAIN YOUR BRAIN TO ACHIEVE SUCCESS**: Download at https://ditchyourgrind.gopages.co/train-your-brain-ebook

About The Author

My passion is to help women entrepreneurs, who feel frustrated they have not been able to make the difference for others they want to make. My "Go For YES" fun 4-step formula makes it possible for them to attract their ideal audience, solve the problems of their audience, increase their income, and leave a positive legacy that lives on long after they are gone.

CONTACT INFORMATION

Stacey Hall
Success with Stacey Hall
https://www.facebook.com/staceyhall1
LinkedIn: https://www.linkedin.com/in/staceyhall1/
staceyhall.chitobe@gmail.com
http://successwithstaceyhall.com/

Conclusion and Powerful Takeaways

REMEMBERING ANNA

Life is short. Most of us spend our lives in a cloud of neurosis and self-judgement worrying about inconsequential things. We spend our lives holding ourselves back from finding out what our lives could be if we just let go of fear. Anna Forbes had more light and promise in her than she ever realized. When she first approached Powerful Women Today in 2021, she wanted to grow her budding business. But she was not sure what it could be, she was going through a million options and possibilities in her mind, sometimes leading to paralysis by analysis. We began to break down the perceived barriers. Little by little I got to know her, her background, her work experience, and her level of professional knowledge and sophistication was incredible.

Yet, an extrovert when it came to serving others, she was very shy when it came to speaking about herself, her dreams, and desires. Sometimes we had to turn video off on our calls so she would feel the psychological safety to really say what she thought. I grew to love Anna; her happiness and outright love was palpable. We had plans to shop for downtown condos and visit Yorkville this spring. To sit in a snooty café and watch the world go by while we dreamed BIG!

Anna and her dog Midnight died February 20th, 2022. She was 37 years old, dreaming of a family of her own, dreaming of a legacy through her business and dreaming of all that could be possible within our Powerful Women Today sisterhood.

Anna died with her song, and her best life still in her heart. The world has lost a Rockstar. I am grateful we had a chance to dream together.

WHAT IS YOUR COURAGE PLAN TO BREAK THROUGH YOUR OWN BARRIERS?

Having a roadmap that can be applied to any situation you may find yourself in that takes the courage that you may believe you're lacking. **MARSHA GLEIT** reminds us to double check our understanding of what words mean. What exactly does courage mean: The Webster's dictionary defines courage as *"the ability to do something that frightens one."* It is my belief, which has been proven through my years of experience, that courage is synonymous with self-confidence and self-love and finding the balance within the circle that was described above. I came to this realization as more and more of my clients started their journey towards self-care and becoming the best they could be.

"

> *"When we fear something, we lack the courage to act. But when we want something bad enough, it can be accomplished."*

MARLENE DOSS reminds us that *"I am sharing my story here to encourage you to break through your own barriers, to know that you can face whatever fears you may have and achieve whatever it is that you really want. I truly believe that if I can do it, anyone can! Whatever it is, decide that you are going to do it, step into it in faith and watch as the doors swing wide open. It will take perseverance to stick it out, but know that you are capable and are meant to succeed. The world needs each of us to stop playing small."*

And asked us to reflect:

- ❖ What's playing on your "movie reel"?
- ❖ What do you really want?
- ❖ What is your barrier?

YOUR COURAGE PLAN TO SAY ENOUGH

LEONA KRASNER asks all of us: *"Why do we put up with bad? As in, pretty bad, really bad, in fact. Crying yourself to bed more nights than not. Pain—emotional or physical. Hurting and feeling as though you aren't enough. But the alternative—loneliness—often feels even scarier, until there is just no other option.*

I need you to write down what your idea of the perfect life, and perfect partner, was before you met your current person. What was most important to you then? What is most important to you now? What will you absolutely need in your next relationship, taking particular note of the things that you were putting up with that were hurting you so deeply in your current relationship? And what will you no longer, never again put up with? Really dig deep. Feel the feelings, but write this list."

YOUR COURAGE PLAN TO PAY IT FORWARD.

LAURIE SMITH reminds us that Empowered Women Empower Women. *"As this book is about empowering women, I'll start with how we can help empower other women as strong female leaders.*

First, cheer them on. Promote their ideas. Look around. It won't be hard to identify female colleagues that you admire. Praise them and actively champion their work. Perhaps encourage them to speak up if they don't seem to be heard. If they're more junior than you, mentor them, or recommend them for bigger opportunities.

Second, create opportunities for women to grow and lead. Just as many schools offer women leadership programs, so can businesses of almost any type. There are even job sites designed from which to specifically recruit female leaders. Be creative and look for your own ways to support the effort.

Finally, if it has to be said, make sure you're leaving any pettiness where you left it, in middle school. Don't view another woman as a threat. Compliment her. Her ideas are good. Tell her this. Don't talk poorly to or about her. Find positive things to say behind her back. If she really irritates you, tell your family. Tell your journal."

YOUR COURAGE PLAN TO NO REGRETS.

SALLIE WAGNER puts it best. *"It is all your choice. The most common regret is: I wish I'd had the courage to live a life true to* *myself, not the life others expected of me. [https://bronnieware. com]*

As if to say, if only I'd had the courage to live the life that makes me come alive. If only I'd had the courage to be the main character of my own life, rather than a non-player character.

You see, as people looked back over their lives, with the clarity that comes from facing their own mortality, they realized that they hadn't lived out their dreams. And they also realized that it was because of their own choices."

> **"**
> *"Many of us experience regrets throughout our lives—not only at the end of our lives."*

YOUR COURAGE PLAIN TO RECOGNIZE THAT: FEAR IS A WARNING SIGN

STACEY HALL is someone who goes against the current by telling you to stay and go with your current. *"Going back to the experience that caused you to feel extreme stress, you may remember that you began to feel you were "getting bent out of shape" by attempting to do what would be required to be successful.*

You probably felt anxious and worried, which is what caused you to slow down—you were fearful about what was ahead if you continued in this direction. Fear is what other people tell you to face to be successful. Facing fear and doing whatever it is anyway is supposed to be a sign of courage.

I don't say that. I say fear is an indication that something about what lies ahead is outside of our comfort zone - that we cannot see a way to remain in alignment with our core values and priorities. Fear tells us to check in with ourselves to make sure what we are moving towards is in alignment with our values and purpose."

STOP PLAYING NICE! YOU'RE A BADASS LADY

I read **SIOBHAN CUNNINGHAM'S** chapter many times while finalizing this book. Her words haunted me: *"The time and energy that I spent finding the perfect solutions to the wrong problems slowed down my progress. I knew I was on the right track, but nothing ever felt like the next best step for what I wanted to do and who I wanted to serve. I kept asking myself, "What am I doing wrong?"*

Finally, my heart led me to the truth. I was afraid to fail again. It was time for me to confront the most uncomfortable feelings about myself. At that moment, I stopped being the good girl who puts others before herself and started being a badass lady who handles adulting like a boss. My Breaking Baddie moment. The moment I stopped caring about what people would think of me and leaned into the possibilities of learning from failure to pursue the lifestyle of my dreams."

May you find the courage to fail your way to your best life.

Join us a life of empowerment is one "Hell Yes" of a ride.

www.powerfulwomentoday.com

> **❝**
> *"The cave you fear to enter*
> *holds the treasures you seek"*
> —Joseph Campbell

Learn More

We created a companion guide to *"Awaken Your Emotional and Financial Independence"* in you and to show you how small changes lead to big results.

We wanted our journey of empowerment to inspire you to take action and start a journey of self-discovery and action.

www.powerfulwomentoday.com

We personally invite you to join our communities on social media
https://www.facebook.com/powerfulwomentoday/
https://www.linkedin.com/in/carolinabillings/
https://www.youtube.com/powerfulwomentoday/

Our hashtags
#PowerfulWomenToday
#PWTProud #StrongerTogether

For further information, please email at info@powerfulwomentoday.com.

CONTACT INFORMATION

Powerful Women Today
3 Centre St. Suite 202, Markham, ON L3P 3P9, Canada
Email: info@powerfulwomentoday.com

Websites:
PowerfulWomenToday.com
PWTSpeakersAssociation.com
PWTCoaching.com
PWTPublishing.com

OTHER BOOKS BY PWT PUBLISHING

Find books by PWT Publishing on Amazon
or anywhere books are sold

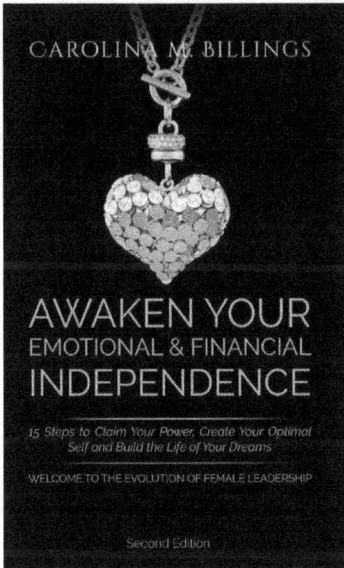

**Awaken Your Emotional
& Financial Independence**

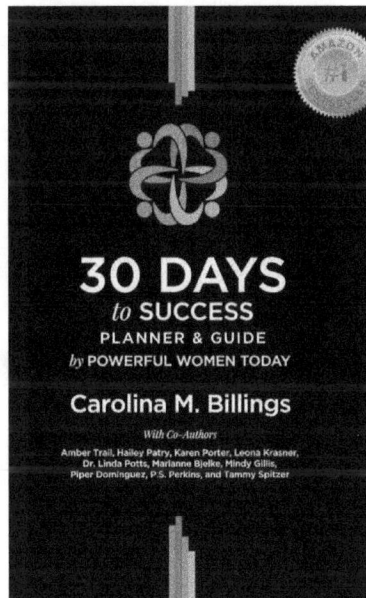

**30 Days to Success
Planner & Guide**

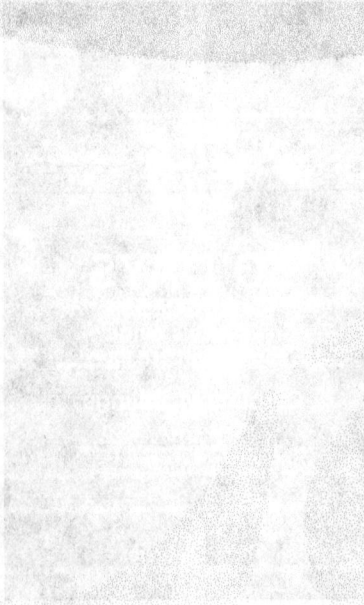

www.ingramcontent.com/pod-product-compliance
Lightning Source LLC
Chambersburg PA
CBHW070908030426

42336CB00014BA/2338